WORK LIKE A SPY

WORK LIKE A

SPY

J. C. Carleson

Portfolio / Penguin

To K. Both of you.

PORTFOLIO / PENGUIN
Published by the Penguin Group
Penguin Group (USA) Inc., 375 Hudson Street, New York, New York 10014, U.S.A.
Penguin Group (Canada), 90 Eglinton Avenue East, Suite 700, Toronto, Ontario,
Canada M4P 2Y3 (a division of Pearson Penguin Canada Inc.)
Penguin Books Ltd, 80 Strand, London WC2R 0RL, England
Penguin Ireland, 25 St. Stephen's Green, Dublin 2, Ireland (a division of Penguin
Books Ltd)
Penguin Group (Australia), 707 Collins Street, Melbourne, Victoria 3008, Australia
(a division of Pearson Australia Group Pty Ltd)
Penguin Books India Pvt Ltd, 11 Community Centre, Panchsheel Park,
New Delhi – 110 017, India
Penguin Group (NZ), 67 Apollo Drive, Rosedale, Auckland 0632, New Zealand (a
division of Pearson New Zealand Ltd)
Penguin Books, Rosebank Office Park, 181 Jan Smuts Avenue, Parktown North 2193,
South Africa
Penguin China, B7 Jaiming Center, 27 East Third Ring Road North, Chaoyang
District, Beijing 100020, China

Penguin Books Ltd, Registered Offices:
80 Strand, London WC2R 0RL, England

First published in 2013 by Portfolio / Penguin,
a member of Penguin Group (USA) Inc.

10 9 8 7 6 5 4 3 2 1

Copyright © J. C. Carleson, 2013
All rights reserved

LIBRARY OF CONGRESS CATALOGING IN PUBLICATION DATA

Carleson, J. C.
Work like a spy : business tips from a former CIA officer / J.C. Carleson.
    p. cm.
Includes index.
ISBN 978-1-59184-353-5
1. Management. 2. Espionage—Psychological aspects. I. Title.
HD31.C3437 2013
658—dc23
                    2012036951

Printed in the United States of America
Set in Adobe Garamond Pro
Designed by Elyse Strongin, Neuwirth & Associates, Inc.

CONTENTS

A Note from the Author

Working as an undercover CIA officer more or less ruins your chances of ever being satisfied again in a more traditional job. So when I started thinking about leaving the agency after spending nearly a decade as a clandestine service officer, I found it hard to imagine going back to a job that required normal business attire, had a predictable schedule, and didn't ever involve the use of an alias. Given the choice, I'd pick a war zone assignment over a cubicle any day.

And yet it was clear to me that I had reached a plateau in my career and it was time to make a change. Still, quitting my job as a case officer for the Central Intelligence Agency was a difficult choice. Sure, a clandestine career has plenty of drawbacks: mind-numbing bureaucracy, too much time living out of a suitcase, constant lies to friends and family. But working for the CIA presents opportunities and challenges that no other employer in the world can match. It can be fabulously rewarding, and although Hollywood's depiction of a CIA career is 98 percent inaccurate, it does have its share of glamorous moments, as well as its pulse-quickening, adrenaline-rushing ones. But I had come to a point where further career advancement would have required personal sacrifices that I wasn't willing to make. I had a family I wanted to see more. I wanted to engage in normal conversations at cocktail parties and backyard barbecues without having to excuse myself whenever the inevitable "and what do *you* do?" question arose. The globe-trotting that had previously seemed a wonderful adventure on the government's dime now had me shudder at the thought of yet *another* international flight and yet *another* night in *another* hotel room. I have absolutely no regrets about my time in the CIA, but I wanted my life and my identity back.

I had a choice: I could make a new career for myself within the clandestine service in a headquarters management role, or I could quit and rejoin the "civilian" world. There was some comfort in the thought of sticking with the CIA, albeit in a different capacity, but the truth is that I share the field officer's aversion to becoming a cog in the headquarters machine.

I had plenty of other skills besides espionage, I told myself. Before joining the CIA, I had hopped from one corporate job to the next. An Ivy League degree and the heady days before the dot-com bubble burst had made it possible for me to dabble in various industries in various capacities, always changing jobs quickly before boredom set in. Granted, I never found a position or a company that I enjoyed for more than about a year's time, but I gained plenty of experience in the normal world outside of the clandestine service.

Upon dusting off my decade-old pre-CIA résumé in search of updatable skills, then, I was surprised to discover that my career in the CIA had taught me more valuable, business-applicable skills than all of my previous corporate positions combined. Granted, not all of my clandestine skills were directly transferable—at least not without the risk of a prison sentence—but they were not nearly as esoteric as I had originally assumed.

This thought process and personal career exploration ultimately led to my decision to write this book. Moreover, I realized that although the CIA employs a constant stream of contractors from the outside world, the outside world rarely gets to benefit from the experience of clandestine service officers. That is, in part, simply because there aren't many of us floating around the private sector. It also stems from the fact that even after leaving the agency, many people find it hard (or inadvisable) to give up their cover stories. Widely broadcasting a previous career as a CIA officer can invite very strong reactions, ranging from curious to confrontational.

Even as this book started to take shape in my mind, though, I hesitated. I had no desire to write a "tell-all"; I don't have any intention of leaking classified information or revealing data that could compromise any person or operation associated with the CIA. Former insiders who leak information are much reviled inside the agency, and I hated the idea that anyone would lump me in with that group. In addition to getting my manuscript approved by the CIA's internal review board prior to publication, as required of all former employees, then, I also set about writing this book very carefully. On the one hand, I truly believe that the corporate world can learn a great deal from some of the practices within the clandestine world, and I wanted readers to have the benefit of examples and anecdotes that illustrate the points discussed in the book. On the other hand, I know how to keep a secret—and there is a great deal of information classified as top secret for very good reason.

My goal in this book is to walk the fine line of sharing enough information for the material to be usable and useful, without giving away any sources or methods that could jeopardize past or present operations. Particularly in the early chapters, therefore, I sometimes rely on hypothetical examples to introduce broad concepts. This does not mean that the examples are untrue or fabricated—just that I used composite characters and situations, and changed the details enough to obscure the underlying people and places. All of the examples that describe my personal experiences are very much true, and very much my own. Again, however, I endeavored to eliminate any detail that could lead to the identification of the other people or places involved.

Purists and former colleagues may object to my interchangeable use of various phrases. So to put the sticklers at ease, let's set the record straight: CIA officers are *not* "spies." A spy is someone who commits espionage against his or her nation. CIA officers *recruit* spies. Yet in the pages of this book I make use of a whole slew of phrases to describe CIA officers from the National Clandestine Service: case officer, clandestine service officer, undercover officer, and—yes—once or twice, even spy and spook. All but the last two are accurate, and those are only used flippantly for effect.

The bottom line is that I very much enjoyed my undercover career, and I have immense respect for my former colleagues. This book is intended to share just a small fraction of the wonderful tricks of the clandestine trade with an outside world that stands to benefit.

Part One

INTRODUCTION TO THE CLANDESTINE WORLD

CHAPTER ONE

Clandestine Concepts Go Corporate: Basic Principles of Intelligence Collection

In the summer of 2003 I had the dubious distinction of being part of the CIA's weapons of mass destruction search team in Iraq. I arrived in Baghdad during an awkward time of investigative limbo—the administration's official position was still that there were weapons of mass destruction hidden in or near Iraq. The evidence, however, was increasingly pointing to the opposite conclusion. The CIA team's orders were a half-vague, half-desperate command to "leave no stone unturned" in our search.

Shortly after my arrival I was asked to look into a suspect biological weapons facility. It was a promising target; we had incriminating satellite imagery and in-depth analysis of the facility's communications with numerous organizations all thought to be part of Iraq's WMD program. The facility, which was run by a PhD biochemist, was under heavy armed guard.

I worked with my military counterparts to develop a plan to raid the site, and several days later I was en route in my first military convoy. I was in an armored car at the center of the convoy, accompanied by my interpreter—a sweet-tempered, slightly nervous woman—and a heavy protective detail manned by Blackwater personnel. Another armored car carried technical specialists who had the ability to run field analyses on any biological weapons (BW) samples that we might collect.

I waited in the car while the compound was secured, then two heavily armed Blackwater guards escorted me into the site's outer courtyard once the facility's guards had been disarmed. The raid was unexpected, and as I entered the compound there must have been a hundred curious—and frightened—eyes on me from the men who had been ordered out of the building, searched for weapons, and made to wait in a secured corner of the courtyard.

A distinguished-looking woman emerged from the building. She appeared shaken, but she remained composed as she introduced herself as the director of the facility and asked more politely than the situation probably warranted how she could be of assistance. I introduced myself in vague terms, using an alias.

I accepted her invitation for tea and started to follow her into her office. The lead Blackwater guard pulled me roughly back, hissing that it had not yet been secured. I peered in, saw nothing but a typical office, and entered anyway.

The director served tea and cookies, and answered all of my questions without hesitation.

The facility was a salt factory. Salt. (Insert your expletive of choice here.) Salt! She pulled out a product sample and offered to taste it in my presence.

She explained everything. The middle-of-the-night deliveries to Iraqi military and prison hospitals? Saline solution. Night deliveries because of the summer heat—a common practice.

The clean-room technology in the facility? To produce the sterile saline solution.

The pits dug into the earth behind the building? For harmless runoff. The residue? You guessed it—salt.

Her PhD in biochemistry? Yes, she was overqualified, she admitted, but it was difficult for a woman to find a management position in Iraq.

The armed guards protecting the building? A necessity in postinvasion Iraq to protect against looting.

We had just conducted an armed raid on a salt factory.

The CIA technicians ran tests that confirmed the director's claims. It really was just a salt factory.

I felt like an incredible jerk.

I looked at the crowd of terrified workers who had been corralled into the courtyard by heavily armed Americans, and felt even worse. The director gracefully accepted my apologies, and our convoy departed in shame.

I learned a valuable lesson that day. For all of the sophisticated imagery, technical intercepts, and expert analysis that had been aimed at the supposed biological weapons facility, the true story was only revealed once I marched in and simply asked someone on the inside. What looked incriminating and suspicious on paper suddenly seemed silly and harmless once I sat down for a cup of tea with the facility's director.

For me, the experience was much like looking through a kaleidoscope: one minute you're looking at a blue star pattern, and then with a small *click,* suddenly you're seeing a rainbow-hued diamond pattern instead. Human intelligence—the bread and butter of the Central Intelligence Agency—*is* that click that suddenly transforms the view into something altogether different. There are circumstances in which the right explanation, the inside scoop, the firsthand account can trump even the most sophisticated data analysis. Sometimes you just have to be there to really understand—and if you can't be there, then you need someone who can be there *for* you.

The click factor exists in the corporate world too. You may diligently read all of the business journals, faithfully study your industry's breaking news, be able to recite from memory your competition's last SEC filing, and *still* be missing the whole picture. You need the click that can only be gained from the inside—that can only be gained from well-placed human sources. You need the click to tell you whether you're looking at a WMD facility or a salt factory.

It just so happens that I can teach you how.

Let's be clear, though—this book is not a manual of dirty tricks. I won't tell you how to bug your competitor's boardroom or how to interrogate disloyal employees. There are plenty of firms around that, for a hefty sum per billable hour, will Dumpster dive for revealing documents, obtain phone records, or dig up compromising information about your fellow executives. Often staffed by a combination of former feds and ex-CIA spooks, these firms can take care of your less than savory business needs.

This book is different. It will teach you to use techniques from the clandestine world to help you legitimately succeed in the business world—as an individual and as an organization. Specifically, this book will show you the value of using classic spy methods to better understand and to better manipulate (more on *that* loaded term later) your customers, your competition, and your suppliers. You won't need a trench coat, a false mustache, or any fancy listening devices. You'll just need a lot of common sense, good intuition, a strong strategy, and firm ethical parameters to successfully use the techniques described.

Yet while this book may not be a manual of dirty tricks, neither is it a Pollyannaish recitation of basic business fundamentals wrapped in a layer of patriotic service. Espionage relies on a lot of loaded terms that I will use frequently: manipulation, exploitation, trapping, and elicitation, among others. And yet CIA officers are, for the most part, some of the most ethical, patriotic, principled people you will ever meet. They are simply adept at using controversial methods when the stakes are high in order to obtain a positive outcome.

So on that note, remember the SWOT model that we all learned in Business 101? (That's an analysis of strengths, weaknesses, opportunities, and threats, for those of you who slept through class that day.) For the purposes of this book, forget about the S part of the model. Building the strengths of your company is not the theme here; you can figure out how to build a better widget on your own time. This book will focus more on weakness—human weakness, that is. And by taking a walk on the clandestine side, you will come to live and breathe opportunities and threats. I will not be encouraging anyone to whiteboard their thoughts, conduct brainstorming sessions, or create columns or graphs of their data. To be successful in the clandestine world you need to *intuitively* recognize both an opportunity and a threat, and then be able to respond reflexively.

To get you started thinking like a spy, I have broken this book into three parts. The first is an introduction to the basic skill sets required in the clandestine world. The chapters in this part identify and distill various techniques used by CIA officers that can also be used by anyone—at any level—in the workplace. Various exercises are included to help readers fine-tune their spy skills.

The second part takes a step back to look at the bigger picture of how lessons from the CIA can benefit entire organizations. The chapters in this section discuss clandestine skills and techniques that can be applied *within* an organization in order to improve performance and outcomes.

The third part of the book returns the focus to the individual level, and is designed to teach readers to apply their newfound skills to specific business situations. The chapters in this section discuss the use of clandestine techniques as they relate to customers, suppliers, and competitors.

Once again, the purpose of this book is not to teach, encourage, or otherwise promote corporate espionage or any type of unethical practice. Instead, it is intended to share some of the techniques used by loyal and dedicated intelligence officers that can also benefit the corporate world.

THE BASICS

I mentioned earlier that the bread and butter of the clandestine world is the collection of human intelligence. In this context, the term "intelligence" refers to secret information; human intelligence means that the information is obtained directly from a person, as opposed to getting it via technical means—hacking into a computer or tapping a phone, for example. CIA officers get paid to obtain secret information from the people who have access to it. To put it more bluntly, CIA officers get paid to steal secrets from other people.

At this point, you might be wondering what this has to do with business—legitimate, *legal* business, in particular. After all, a company's proprietary information, while important, is not exactly on par with information about a hostile nation's secret biological weapons arsenal. And most of you (I hope) don't want to *steal* another company's proprietary information anyway. So why bother reading a business book written by a former spy?

Because, quite simply, the techniques used in the clandestine world are broadly applicable, universal methods for getting what you want from other people.

In the business setting, you may be seeking a new job, a promotion, a big sale, or a regulatory ruling in your company's favor.

Whatever it is that you seek, *someone* has the power to give. This book will teach you how to more effectively get what you need to succeed.

JAMES BOND MEETS THE BOND MARKET

The synergy between clandestine techniques, or *tradecraft,* as it is often called, and the corporate world may be best demonstrated by comparing examples. We'll start with a classic espionage scenario:

> After years of unsuccessfully trying to penetrate the nuclear program of a hostile rogue nation, John, a mid-career CIA officer, finally struck gold—one of the chief architects of the nuclear program had been arrested for drunk driving while on vacation with his family in a cooperative country. By taking advantage of the nuclear official's detention and embarrassment, plus offering a hefty reward for his cooperation, John was able to persuade the official to defect to the United States and to provide invaluable top-secret information about the rogue nation's weapons program. It didn't take long for this coup to have a ripple effect. Knowing that it was only a matter of time until the program was dismantled or worse, a number of other key officials and scientists abandoned the now-compromised program in the hope of both avoiding prosecution and obtaining substantial rewards like their former colleague. Ultimately, the loss of the key officials and scientists decimated the country's capabilities, and the fledgling nuclear program ground to a halt.

Now imagine a parallel (albeit less dramatic) scenario in the business world:

> In spite of its high-caliber research and development department, high-tech Company X was continually upstaged by competing Company Y's ability to beat its new products to market. In a cutthroat niche in which being the first to market was critical to a product's success, Company X just couldn't seem to get ahead, in spite of an arguably better product. Finally, Company X's vice president of human resources struck gold. After learning that Company Y's most senior program manager had argued bitterly with the company's president, Company X quickly made him a job offer that he couldn't refuse. The program manager's defection soon produced a ripple effect: it turned out that he was much revered by his staff, so he also brought with him a talented team of loyal subordinates. The group desertion decimated Company Y's program management team and brought both talented employees and a competitive advantage to Company X.

Both examples involve a time-sensitive opportunity to lure a key player from the competition. In each scenario, the time-sensitive opportunity was only known because the principal actor (CIA officer John and Company X's vice president of HR, respectively) had established intelligence networks that alerted them to the opportunities. Then, in both cases, not only did the principal player draft one individual over to his side, but he also managed to recruit that one *key* individual who could cause a domino effect of defections. In both scenarios, the collection and subsequent use of human intelligence led to a key recruitment that strengthened one side to the detriment of the other.

The parallel examples and synergies between the clandestine and the corporate worlds are endless. Some of the other business needs that can be addressed by the techniques of espionage include:

- Understanding what your customer really wants
- Positioning yourself next in line for promotion
- Identifying supply-chain problems before they become your problems
- Preventing corporate espionage against your company
- Motivating employees during tough times for your company
- Determining who you can really trust
- Identifying team members who will help you to succeed
- Dealing with a crisis

This list could go on and on. Ultimately, the purpose of this book is to teach you to think and act like a spy, and to use human intelligence collection techniques in order to succeed.

PROFILE OF A SPY

If you don't happen to resemble James Bond, you may be skeptical of this book's ability to teach you clandestine tradecraft. Rest assured, there are very few people who look like Sean Connery walking through the halls of the CIA's Langley headquarters. In fact, the most common reaction of new CIA officers reporting to duty on their first day of work is . . . disappointment.

Almost all new hires to the clandestine service exhibit the same behaviors. We show up excited and nervous; many of us didn't sleep well the night before. This isn't like any other first day of work; this is the first day of work at *the CIA*! We make our way uncertainly through the complex security process required just to get in the door. We don't make eye contact with anyone else, because we aren't sure whether it's appropriate to meet and mingle as one might at any other new-employee orientation. Few people shake hands; almost no one introduces themselves—we don't know whether we're allowed to share our names. So we lurk quietly, sipping our coffee, observing everyone else in the new-employee orientation room. And we see . . . ordinary people. We usually start to feel a little silly at this point for even having thought that our fellow employees might look like Hollywood's version of a spy, but we're still surprised by just how average the people around us appear. But appearing ordinary is precisely the point. After all, would someone who looks like Brad Pitt or Angelina Jolie be able to cross borders without drawing attention? Could someone truly remarkable in appearance ever be able to operate in stealth mode?

Yet although CIA officers are for the most part surprisingly ordinary in appearance, their remarkable qualities become more apparent once you get a chance to talk with them for a while. Successful spies rely on their personalities, not their looks. A good CIA officer is charismatic without being flashy, inquisitive without being nosy, friendly without being boisterous, smart without being pedantic, and confident without seeming arrogant. Above all, a good spy is a *great* listener.

A good CIA officer starts conversations easily, and has a talent for guiding a seemingly idle chat toward a topic of interest. Somewhere along the way you'll find that *you* are doing most of the talking, allowing the spy to draw information from you effortlessly. And if you bump into that CIA officer later, don't be surprised if he or she has an uncanny ability to remember the details you shared.

Good CIA officers have great personalities. They're charming, witty, and extremely persuasive. But they're not necessarily the "life of the party." They're not usually the ones cracking jokes or buying rounds of drinks. They *are* the ones who draw you into a very pleasant, long conversation, though, and you will often find yourself uncharacteristically sharing deeply personal information with them.

THE GOAL

Of course, applicants to the CIA are screened for these personality variables. Job candidates are selected, in part, for their ability to converse, charm, think on their feet, and persuade. Applicants go through numerous batteries of personality tests, and are carefully screened by trained psychologists. But not all of a good CIA officer's skills are innate. Our training introduces us to techniques designed to elicit information gently and gracefully from a reluctant source. We are taught to use our natural abilities to pursue a specific goal.

This training, which will be addressed in the next chapter, can benefit you and your organization as well. Anyone can learn to be a better listener, a more influential speaker, and a generally more persuasive person. Whether you are an engineer, a lawyer, a sales rep, or an accountant, you can benefit from training in clandestine methods. Even if your interpersonal skills have long been buried under mountains of paperwork, the drudgery of an eighty-hour workweek, or the infighting of a brutally competitive workplace, I can teach you how to better listen, elicit, and manipulate yourself into success.

CHAPTER TWO

Secret Agent Boot Camp:
Developing Your Operational Instincts

C IA clandestine service officers are the world's best sales-people—truly. Consider the fact that it is an officer's job to persuade people to commit espionage—to violate oaths, allegiances, and the law, often betraying friends, colleagues, and even family along the way. By definition, the stakes are always extremely high, since in many cases the penalty for committing espionage is life imprisonment or death. The spy game is serious business indeed, for all participants.

Wouldn't it be nice, then, if there was one tried-and-true method for persuading people to secretly provide sensitive information to the U.S. government? Obviously there isn't, or else we would not be suffering from ongoing, critical intelligence gaps. And yet every day CIA officers are out there, working undercover to slowly but surely eke out the bits and pieces of information that might thwart the next planned terrorist attack, uncover a hidden nuclear arsenal, or unmask the next Aldrich Ames.

Generally speaking, the recruitment cycle used by CIA officers to find new sources is as follows: spot, assess, develop, recruit, then handle (the somewhat pessimistic inside term for "manage") spies. Completing this cycle can take days or it can take years; sometimes the process is smooth and natural, and sometimes you don't know whether you are going to end up with a recruited spy or a stint in a third world prison cell when you finally pop the big question.

CIA officers often begin to truly care about the person they have recruited. In these cases the officer respects the individual's motives and takes very personally the obligation to ensure the recruit's safety. Other times we may despise the "asset," as he or she is coldly referred to in CIA parlance: we steel ourselves before every encounter in order to maintain the charade of caring about the person, and we have to remind ourselves constantly that though the asset may be reprehensible, he has access to critically important information.

The process of recruiting someone to commit espionage is inevitably complicated by language and cultural differences, plus neverending logistical and security challenges. Yet while each recruitment has its own distinct story, there are several universal elements that serve as the building blocks for each step of the recruitment cycle:

- Targeting
- Strategic elicitation
- Corroboration
- Development of trust and rapport

CIA clandestine service officers go through months and months of training to hone their skills in these areas. Elaborate live scenarios based on actual events are staged with increasing levels of difficulty and consequences so that fledgling officers can perfect the recruitment cycle, with all of its stumbling points and inevitable psychological drama. Because the building blocks are equally valuable in the corporate world, this chapter provides readers with a series of exercises based on the principles underlying all CIA operations. Each lesson provides skills that can be employed in the private sector, both within your own organization and in the greater competitive marketplace. The techniques, as you will soon see, are not just relevant to the spy world. These are universal skills and strategies that can be used in any context.

TARGETING

Targeting is the two-pronged process of obtaining information that will enable you to get close to your person or organization of interest. First, you seek to identify *who* can get you what you need. Second, you formulate a "hook" that you can use to facilitate contact with that person.

In the world of espionage, targeting is focused on identifying specific individuals who have access to information of interest to the U.S. government. Here's a hypothetical example:

> United States authorities suspected the existence of a terrorist sleeper cell in a European capital; according to an anonymous tip, the group planned to attack the U.S. embassy within the next year. Several possible members were identified, but because the terrorists used strict operational security—avoiding phone calls and electronic communication—intelligence officials remained unable to confirm the plans or intentions of the suspect cell. Without concrete evidence of a pending attack, European law enforcement officials were un-

able to act. The only chance of penetrating the cell was to recruit someone in, or close to, the terrorist organization's inner circle. CIA targeting experts quickly worked to identify possible recruitment candidates. The list of possible informants included family members, neighbors, and a wide assortment of individuals who had ongoing contact with the suspected terrorists. Ultimately, a CIA officer recruited the landlord of the apartment building where the suspect terrorists lived. The landlord, who was happy to help once he learned that the cell members were possibly storing explosive materials in his property, was able to provide information about the comings and goings of the cell members, and physical access to their residence. This access yielded sufficient incriminating evidence to justify the arrest of the cell members. Once in jail, a junior cell member confessed that the group had planned to carry out its attack within a month.

In this case, the "who" was an individual who had physical proximity to the terrorist cell members, but no ideological affiliation with the group. Now let's see how targeting can be used in a corporate setting:

Margaret, the president of a five-person software company, knew that there was a large potential market for her company's product in Asia. The problem was that the company had no in-house expertise in international sales development. Unfortunately, without a significant increase in sales, Margaret couldn't justify hiring anyone qualified to take her company overseas. She was discouraged by the high commissions demanded by so-called international facilitators, and she had already been burned once by an unsuccessful attempt to partner with another company that had made false promises about its ability to tap into the Asian market. In desperation, Margaret convened a staff meeting and instructed all of her employees to network as widely as they possibly could; she noted that the future of the company depended on their ability to find the right expertise. By the end of the day, Margaret had a list of potential candidates. The individuals on the list ranged from the receptionist's cousin, who was an international trade lawyer in Bangkok, to a number of impressively credentialed individuals from various employees' college alumni associations. Ultimately, one of the alumni contacts agreed to work as a consultant for Margaret for very favorable terms in exchange for the promise of a significant bonus upon meeting an ambitious overseas sales goal.

In the corporate example, the "who" yielded by the targeting efforts was someone with significant international sales development experience who also had a personal connection to the company that made him more willing to accept a consultancy with an uncertain payout.

Targeting can also go far beyond the type of strategic networking described in the corporate example, though. In many business scenarios, the "who" may be obvious, while the "hook" is not. In all likelihood, you know exactly *who* you need to impress in order to get the job, the promotion, or the big sale. If that's the case, then targeting can also be used to determine how to get the critical first meeting with that key decision maker, and also what to use to influence the meeting's outcome.

Targeting How-to: Find Your Hook

> Karyn, a second-tour officer posted in a South American country, needed to move quickly. She had been assigned a target months ago, but hadn't managed to make any progress. The target simply wasn't approachable. He didn't travel, he rarely socialized, he didn't accept meetings with unknown entities, and his home was patrolled by private security guards who kept uninvited visitors away. Karyn thought that she had exhausted all of her options for establishing initial contact when she happened upon a critical piece of information: the target's youngest son was applying to universities in the United States.
>
> Armed with this hook, Karyn easily arranged a meeting with the target under the guise of a private foundation offering scholarships to international students. This time, the target eagerly accepted a personal meeting with Karyn. While she initially used a deceptive pretense for the meeting, she gradually revealed her true affiliation after several meetings, and ultimately recruited the elusive target.

CIA officers spend a great deal of time formulating personalized hooks for their targets. A proper hook contains three elements:

- A reason to meet once
- A reason to connect
- A reason to continue to meet

A good hook allows a case officer to establish a mutually beneficial relationship quickly—even if this relationship is based on deception.

In the corporate world, you obviously don't want to start new business relationships with a lie. Therefore, targeting in the private sector is, fundamentally, just focused research designed to uncover your target's hook. In the age of the Internet it's easy to find information that arms you with a reason to approach a person. For example, prior to a sales call at a potential new customer's office, a meeting with executives of your company, or a series of job interviews, research the participants. If you don't know who will be attending the meetings, find out. This is less awkward than it may sound; you can always inquire with the excuse that you plan to bring specifically addressed materials. (Don't be sloppy here—if you give a reason for inquiring, follow through. Have the preaddressed materials ready to hand to the participants, or else run the risk of appearing flighty.)

Online social networking—both a blessing and a curse for intelligence officers—means that more personal information, and more potential hooks, are publicly available than ever before. Although these sites tend to be skewed toward the younger crowd, as opposed to the gray-haired executive set, don't dismiss their value. Even if your company's CEO doesn't have a Facebook page, he or she may be actively involved in charities, alumni organizations, clubs, or professional organizations. All of these affiliations tend to leave an easily researched public footprint that can readily give you insight into the where and the how to meet and "recruit" the person who can get you what you want.

Using this information successfully sometimes requires a subtle hand; you don't want to appear to be stalking your target, since nothing will get you turned down for a job or a sale faster than being a creepy and constant presence. But mentioning in your cover letter that you recently heard your target speak at a charity event, for example, provides an excellent opportunity to establish common ground, and to be complimentary in a professionally appropriate manner.

Since this chapter is titled "Secret Agent Boot Camp," I feel compelled to provide exercises to help you hone your clandestine skills. Even if you don't want to actually complete the challenges, I encourage you to at least go through them mentally. The exercises are as much about providing you with a new strategy and mind-set as they are about learning skills that are used every day by CIA officers.

Targeting Exercise

Let's begin with an easy exercise. In order for you to become more thorough and intuitive at targeting, we'll start out by working backward. Pick three people you know well, but who don't know one another. Ideally, each person will be from a different socioeconomic background and a different geographic area. Try to choose three people who are very different in their interests, occupations, and habits.

Next, make a separate list for each target, detailing how and where you might go about making contact with them if you were not already acquainted. Start with the basics. List items might include:

- Church or place of worship
- Club memberships
- Place of employment
- Hobbies
- Neighborhood
- Professional organizations
- Alumni affiliations, including fraternities or sororities
- Online group memberships

Don't be afraid to get creative. Do you have any mutual acquaintances who could introduce you? List all of them (extra credit if you can go beyond one degree of separation). Do your targets have children? If so, they may be frequent visitors to sporting events, school activities, playgrounds, and other children's activities. Of course, you'd likely be met with little more than resentment and irritation for trying to make a sale at your target's daughter's soccer match, but targeting can be used not just to locate and approach but also to establish commonalities once a more benign or appropriate contact is made.

Now compare your three lists. Are you surprised by the number of possible targeting venues for each person? Which of your three targets appears to be the easiest to approach? Which has the largest public footprint? Because, as part of this exercise, you actually know each of your targets well, consider how they would respond to being approached at or via your list items. Which means of establishing connection would most likely yield a positive response? Which would likely yield a negative response? What is the most subtle, natural means of making contact with each of your targets?

The latter part of this exercise—considering the potential reaction to a given approach—is just as important as being able to generate a lengthy list of targeting venues. Without this consideration, you could engineer the perfect introduction, yet risk burning bridges forever if you are perceived as overly aggressive, unprofessional, or intrusive.

Now that you have gotten the hang of targeting using individuals you already know well, you can apply the same technique to your professional life. Use targeting principles to identify as many people as possible who can get you closer to your goals, whether that means a new job, a new client, a new sale, or a new product.

STRATEGIC ELICITATION

24

Hollywood often depicts CIA officers engaged in harsh interrogation sessions to get the information that they need from their sources. The reality is that CIA officers spend a great deal of time perfecting a far more subtle and nonviolent technique—they use *elicitation* rather than *interrogation*. The distinction is important. Strategic elicitation involves getting the answers that you need without ever directly asking the question. You wouldn't march up to a competitor and bluntly ask him or her to reveal trade secrets, would you? To do so would bring ridicule at best, and possibly even professional censure or blacklisting.

Strategic elicitation involves asking benign, nonalerting questions that eventually reveal information that likely would not have been given had you asked directly. This does not mean "tricking" anyone into answering a question; rather, it involves obtaining partial bits of information that you can, unbeknownst to your conversation partner, piece together to provide a complete answer.

In the intelligence world, strategic elicitation is used in network fashion. First, critical intelligence gaps are identified. Second, intelligence analysts formulate the questions that, if answered, could provide answers to fill those gaps. Third, targeting principles are used to identify who might be able to answer the critical questions. Sometimes the information is known to but a single person; other times, there may be a wide variety of people who could shed light on a subject. Generally speaking, the fewer the people who have access to a particular piece of information, the harder it is to get. Finally, intelligence operatives are dispatched to collect the information, in whole or in part, from wherever and whomever they can. The pieces of information are then analyzed in the aggregate, ultimately providing a complete picture.

WORK LIKE A SPY

Consider the following scenario, which demonstrates how the principle of strategic elicitation could be used in the clandestine world:

The intelligence service of a hostile nation was tasked with obtaining information about advances in a strategic missile defense system being developed by the U.S. government. Several clumsy attempts to recruit top U.S. military officials to provide this information resulted in failure and diplomatic sanctions. Stung by the international rebukes, the foreign intelligence service decided to take a more patient and conservative approach. Operatives were dispatched to provide blanket coverage of all of the various parties involved in the development of the defense system. Contact was made with dozens of potential sources of information, including the following individuals: a university professor whose latest research was instrumental to the system's capabilities, a subcontractor who had received technical specifications during the bidding process, a low-level government official who processed paperwork related to the fiscal oversight of the project, a travel agent who made all of the travel arrangements for the various parties attending an important planning meeting, a journalist who had toured a restricted area used for testing the new system for an unrelated story, and a midlevel engineer who had worked on the project but was now seeking other employment. By asking a large number of individuals each a few key questions that in and of themselves did not seem suspicious, the hostile nation was able to obtain a staggering amount of key information that jeopardized national security.

Think that this strategy isn't used in the corporate world? Think again. Trade shows, professional networking events, professional organizations, industry-specific conferences or seminars, and even the good old-fashioned golf course can be used to glean information from unsuspecting sources. The information that seemed so harmless in the bar or in the club locker room can end up being much more revealing than intended when analyzed in the aggregate. This threat will be addressed in more detail in the business counterintelligence chapter later in this book.

Strategic elicitation does not, however, need to be a vast undertaking utilizing a small army of intelligence officers. On an individual level, it can be as simple as identifying exactly what information you need, and then preplanning a variety of questions and/or conversational directions that can get you the data. Note that *how* and *what* you ask are both of critical importance. If you are too vague or circumspect, you may never get the information you need. However, being overly blunt or aggressive will also lead to failure.

Strategic elicitation is a particularly ideal technique in two common corporate situations: initial sales meetings and job interviews.

Elicitation in the Real World

Have you ever sat through a job interview where you, the candidate, did almost none of the talking? In my experience (and I am a veteran of an embarrassing number of interviews, since I job-hopped quite a bit before joining the CIA), those were usually the most successful interviews. Quite simply, people like talking about themselves, and they like talking to people who appear interested. It's basic human nature.

Using strategic elicitation in this context, then, involves getting your interviewers to tell *you* what they want to hear. For starters, it is usually easy to glean information about exactly what an interviewer needs to hear from a successful applicant. Imagine the following exchange, in which the applicant uses strategic elicitation at the most basic level:

INTERVIEWER: Before we get started, do you have any questions?

CANDIDATE: Well, you mentioned that you've been with the company for over a decade. Could you tell me a little bit about your career progression here, and what has made you successful?

INTERVIEWER: Interesting question. When I first started, the company didn't even have an in-house marketing capability. I arrived with very little experience, but I was given an overwhelming amount of responsibility. I built the marketing team from scratch, and along the way proved my resourcefulness. I've been very lucky, because senior management allowed me to be creative, and once I had proved myself, they gave me free rein. I'm happy to say that the company has rewarded me for my hard work along the way with regular promotions, which got me to where I am today.

From this very short conversational exchange, the applicant has learned several key elements that the interviewer values: resourcefulness, creativity, initiative, and a willingness to prove one's worth early in the game. Based on the interviewer's own response, the job candidate is now armed with a set of important details that he or she can work into later interview questions. Imagine the next segment of the job interview:

INTERVIEWER: Okay, tell me a little bit about yourself. What makes you a good candidate for this job?

CANDIDATE: Well, I've been with my current employer for several years now, and I've learned a great deal from some truly outstanding mentors. Now I feel ready to stretch my wings a bit and take on a bit more responsibility. I think that you'll find that I'm an out-of-the-box thinker, so I'm looking for a position in a company where I can really make a mark. I'm definitely a self-starter, so I feel as if I'm ready to move into a position that will allow me to prove exactly what I'm capable of.

So what exactly did the candidate reveal about himself here? Absolutely nothing (other than a talent for using corporate clichés). And a skilled interviewer will be waiting for more detail to substantiate all of the candidate's generalized claims and buzzwords. But the candidate has set himself up with a response framework that includes all of the elements the interviewer has already told him are important in order to succeed within the company.

Note that the candidate did not parrot the interviewer's responses verbatim. This is a critical part of strategic elicitation. Had the candidate used the exact verbiage provided by the interviewer ("I'm creative and resourceful, and looking to be rewarded for my hard work"), the answer would have been far too obvious and ham-handed. Instead, the candidate elicited details about what the interviewer thinks are critical for success, processed them, and then used those details to craft his own substantively similar but not identical response.

In order to practice your strategic elicitation skills, try the following exercise, which can be quite challenging for all but the most outgoing individuals.

Strategic Elicitation Exercise

The last exercise let you off easily by allowing you to practice targeting using information about people you already know well. To practice your strategic elicitation skills, however, it's time to exit your comfort zone and practice on a complete stranger. If you're really up for a challenge, pick a practice target who comes from a different culture than you, and who maybe isn't even fully fluent in your native language. These are challenges faced by CIA officers every day! Not sure where to find your target? Try dining at an ethnic restaurant or shopping at an ethnic grocery store staffed by employees from a culture you don't know well, and then strike up a conversation. As a customer, you have a built-in reason to initiate an exchange.

Before starting out, identify one or two questions that you would like answered during the course of your conversation. Here's the hard part: you can't ask for the information directly, and it needs to be totally unrelated to the nature of your business transaction. No fair asking the waitress at the Thai restaurant if the pad kee mao is spicy! Your quest does not have to be difficult or complex; it simply needs to be totally divergent from your task at hand. For example, find a way to get the bartender at the Russian restaurant to tell you his favorite color. Or try to learn what kind of car the butcher at the halal grocery store drives.

This can be a very difficult task, and can even be excruciating for those of you who tend to be shy. Bluntly asking your intended question would be awkward and out of context, so you need to work out a reason in advance to elicit your information in the context of your natural encounter.

The strategic elicitation exercise above may seem awkward and forced, because you are attempting to segue from the natural flow of a normal interaction (simply entering and making a purchase, for example, without extraneous conversation) to eliciting seemingly random information. Don't fret, however. The more consistent your strategic elicitation with your overt interaction, the easier it is to gradually draw out the information you need. So you will likely be pleased to discover that strategic elicitation in the corporate world is actually far easier than the exercise. Getting your customer to tell *you* exactly what she needs to hear in your sales pitch will seem like a cinch if you've already mastered the art of drawing out far more esoteric information from people you don't even know.

Elicitation How-to: Helpful Hints

Some people are harder to chat up than others. So what can you do when you need to elicit information from someone particularly tight-lipped? Here are a few helpful techniques from the clandestine world:

▶ **Give to get.** Having trouble homing in on your goal? Try a strategy that some of us in the clandestine world refer to as "give to get." Talk about your *own* career plans, financial problems, or other personal details. If this is done correctly—in a conversational manner that invites mutual exchange—it naturally draws out reciprocal information from your target. Be careful here, though. If you end up divulging more information about *yourself* than you obtain from your target, then the whole purpose of the strategy is lost.

▶ **Strategic segues.** A sly segue can be a manipulator's best friend. If you are eliciting information that is touchy or sensitive in nature, tread toward your topic lightly by first creating a "segue road map" before you ever talk to your contact. Preplan several relevant, reasonable, and, most important, nonthreatening conversational topics from which you can then appear to effortlessly transition closer and closer to the more sensitive—and more important—real topic of interest. Some topics are so benign and universal—sports and weather, for example—that they can be used as gentle springboards to artfully get your target warmed up for the stickier subjects. Advance planning and a subtle touch are critical here.

▶ **The referral.** A referral from a trusted—or even a neutral, for that matter—third party can do wonders for making your target more comfortable talking to you about sensitive matters. Use this by casually dropping a referral source and a specific insight. For example, something as simple as, "Sheila tells me that you are a veritable patent law guru," conveys to your target that you are more trustworthy by virtue of your connection to a mutual acquaintance, and that you already have some insight into the nature of your target's work, so therefore there must be no harm in further discussing the topic with you.

CORROBORATION

There is usually more to getting the information that you want, however, than just asking the right questions. Sometimes, improving your listening and observational skills yields just as much success as cultivating your elicitation skills. After all, the information you seek may be readily available if you simply pay attention to the right clues. Think about how many meetings you have sat through where participants interrupted one another, talked over other speakers, text messaged, or otherwise mentally checked out? Granted, useless meetings can be a plague to productivity, but a fast-paced corporate culture and constant multitasking has trained many of us to tune out the world (and, along with it, important information) in our constant quest for efficiency. For this reason, CIA officers are trained to use not just verbal elicitation, but also active listening and skillful observation in order to obtain the information they need. Information from different sources can then either corroborate or contradict what you obtain through conversation. When the stakes are high, you can't rely on just one person's version of the facts.

Moreover, some information can't be obtained simply through strategic questioning. For example, motivations. CIA officers are constantly seeking to understand what might motivate a potential spy to agree to hand over top-secret information. Some spies do it for the money, some for ideological reasons, some for revenge, and some just for the thrill of it. There are as many complex sets of motivations as there are spies. It is a CIA officer's job to discern and exploit a potential recruit's vulnerabilities in order to turn them into a motivation to spy.

The ability to identify and understand vulnerabilities and motivations is equally important in the corporate world—whether we're talking about your boss, your client, your peers, or your rivals. Perhaps your boss shows favoritism toward fellow graduates from his college, your client likes to win on the golf course, your colleague plans to retire soon, or your closest rival is a sucker for an attractive blonde. Such knowledge helps you predict behavior, can help you avoid traps, and can enable you to exploit vulnerabilities and motivations to your advantage. This type of information is usually highly personal, though, and can be obtained only through careful observation over time. All the more reason, then, to practice your powers of observation.

Corroboration Exercise I

CIA officers often repeat the mantra "Trust, but verify." Information obtained through one means is good, but the same information corroborated by multiple sources is better. This exercise is a fairly easy one on the surface; the challenge is to absorb the technique and use it on a constant basis.

First, select your target. For this exercise, pick someone whom you interact with on at least a fairly routine basis, but whom you do not know particularly well. A co-worker you do not know on a personal level is an ideal target here.

Your challenge is to obtain a personal detail, and then confirm it two more times, using two different methods of information collection. In other words, you will be collecting the same piece of information three different ways.

A simple place to start is to find out where your target went to college. This is an easy piece of information to obtain during a casual conversation; a colleague isn't likely to be suspicious when you ask where he or she went to school. Next, check out your co-worker's desk; many people have coffee mugs or other school paraphernalia lying around. What about a bumper sticker on his or her car? A class ring, or a T-shirt with a university logo worn on a casual attire day? There's also the Internet; some universities have searchable databases of alumni, and many people now have their résumés and bios posted online for either personal or professional reasons. Finally, you could ask another colleague. Careful—make sure that it's not someone who is likely to report back to your target. You look suspicious if your target learns that you have been asking about him or her.

Once you have collected the same information three different ways, consider it a verified fact. Also, notice how your observational skills increased during the exercise. Be honest—would you normally have noticed the bumper sticker on a distant co-worker's car? And yet you never know when background information that is as easily collectible via an attentive glance can be very useful when the time comes to interact with that colleague.

In addition to learning which school your co-worker attended, try practicing with a few other easy-to-obtain bits of information on other targets. Investigating whether your target has an interest in a specific sport is another easy way to practice—a bike rack on the car, a quote from Lance Armstrong as an e-mail signature, and shaved legs (on a man) all point to an interest in cycling, for example.

To avoid going about this task too bluntly or aggressively, consider yourself to have failed if at any point anyone asks you why you want to know something. If this happens, take a step back, choose a new target and a new piece of information to collect, and proceed more cautiously and patiently.

The point here is not to snoop or collect dirt on your co-workers. The point is to gain an appreciation for the myriad ways that you can obtain information, and to train yourself to absorb the personal details that you otherwise have likely been ignoring every day.

So what about the details and information that can't be gleaned from a T-shirt or a bumper sticker? For example, how can you corroborate a person's character, values, or motivations? How do you determine and then corroborate that a person is trustworthy, or loyal, or talented? You can gather this information over a lengthy period, of course, by observing behavior in different situations and conditions. But if you need to make decisions about people without adequate "time on target," as CIA officers say, then you need to at least train yourself not to make common mistakes.

Business leaders and CIA officers are forced to make snap judgments all the time. For example, CIA officers sometimes have to make an on-the-spot assessment of whether a target is ready to hear a recruitment pitch. An erroneous decision to ask someone to risk their life to spy for the U.S. government can have drastic consequences for the officer (being arrested is *not* considered a career-enhancing move for a clandestine service officer). Similarly, business executives often have to fill important, highly paid positions using only a one-page résumé and a rushed interview to assess candidates. And *all* of us have, at one time or another, scrambled to figure out, off the cuff, exactly what our irate boss/client/spouse needs to hear in order to defuse a bad situation.

To minimize the chance of making the wrong decision in an urgent situation, we use the information that we have at hand. And when there is no data to corroborate the little information that we have, we make assumptions, rely on educated guesses, or sometimes just roll the dice. Unfortunately, taking these chances can often do more harm than good.

Using assumptions in place of corroborating data is toxic to good decision making, especially when you are making a consequential judgment about a person. This is because assumptions about people's characters, values, and motivations are often based on stereotypes. Stereotypes are like mental junk food—filling, but lacking much in the way of nutrients. By using them over time, we become lazy, and we fill in the blanks with the "information" that we pull from our heads, rather than expending the time and effort to obtain facts and corroborating data.

There's not much you can do when decision time rolls around and you need to make a choice without all of the facts. However, at a minimum, you need to understand and account for the mental shortcuts that you tend to take, and the stereotypes and biases you tend to rely on. The following exercise is intended to bring out, and then analyze, the assumptions that *you* tend to make about people.

As an aside, I encourage you to pay *particularly* careful attention to the results of the following exercise if you have ever referred to yourself as a "good judge of character," if you believe that you have a better than average ability to detect lies, or if you consider yourself to be more intuitive than most people. Why? Because, frankly, you are probably wrong. More often than not, these beliefs indicate little more than an overconfidence in one's own assumptions and biases. Fortunately, this tendency can be corrected with a combination of mental discipline and greater self-awareness of internal biases.

Corroboration Exercise 2

As a child, I used to play a game to pass time while waiting for a flight. I would try to guess where the other people in the airport were going based on their attire and characteristics. The people dressed unseasonably were the easiest—passengers wearing shorts in the middle of winter were usually going to a tropical vacation destination (unless, of course, they were already sunburned, in which case they were heading home), and the people wearing heavy parkas were en route to ski destinations. I would try to spot which gate my targets went to, and I won a point for each correct guess.

This exercise is a spin-off of this childhood game. Far from childish, however, these techniques and observations are used by law enforcement and intelligence agencies to develop usable profiles of potential suspects or recruitment targets. Profiling is controversial for good reason, though: depending on how it is used, it can be either a useful tool or a counterproductive assumption. All the more reason to better understand its use!

To start, you will need a situation in which you can observe people prior to making their acquaintance. Parties or weddings are ideal; you can also practice on new co-workers, whom you will eventually get to know better.

First, observe your target from a distance. Pay attention to attire, mannerisms, appearance, facial expressions, body language, and whom he gravitates toward when he interacts with other people. Try to learn as much as you possibly can without actually speaking to your target, but do it reasonably quickly, and try not to get caught staring.

On the basis of your observations, try to establish a "story" for your target. Who is he? Where is he from? Next, make your best guess as to the following:

- Ethnic origins
- Education
- Profession
- Religion
- Income bracket
- Marital status
- Hobbies or activities

Also try to create a quick personality profile of your target. Is he outgoing? Intelligent? Funny? Abrasive? Condescending? Kind? Observe both your target's behavior and the behavior of the people he interacts with to formulate your personality profile from a distance.

For each response that you come up with about your target, try to pinpoint exactly which behavior or other variable led you to your conclusion. For example, did you decide that your target was Scandinavian because of his complexion? Did you decide that his hobby was basketball because of his height? Did you decide that he was a well-off lawyer because of his expensive, conservative suit?

In many cases, identifying the variable that triggered your guess is difficult. Often we base our assumptions on vague impressions or fleeting clues. Identifying which clues *you* tend to use to formulate opinions, however, is a critical part of this exercise. It is important to be able to identify, articulate, and, most of all, *improve* upon our natural tendency to make assumptions.

Next comes the hard part. To the best of your ability, you need to determine the accuracy of your profile. Depending on the context, you can do this directly, by talking to your target and eliciting information, or indirectly, by asking a mutual acquaintance. Be tactful, no matter what you do. Waltzing up and asking a stranger how much money he makes doesn't usually go over well. You can, however, use your strategic elicitation skills to obtain information that will either corroborate or repudiate your profile.

Repeating this exercise with multiple targets will give you a good collection of data to analyze. This analysis of your accuracy is the most important part of the exercise. What did you guess correctly, and what did you miss by a mile? Which clues yield the most accurate guesses? Are you more accurate when you base a guess on a behavior, or on a physical characteristic? Are you more accurate when it comes to profiling men, or women? Young targets, or old? By gaining an appreciation for which variables tend to steer you *wrong,* you can improve your assessment abilities over time.

Generally speaking, the accuracy of our assessments of people tends to increase when we share similarities with our targets. Think about it—you're more likely to identify a class ring if you went to the same university or know someone who did. You're more likely to identify the expensive Italian loafers if you own a pair yourself. Former marines always seem to be able to pick one another out of a crowd, simply based on that special military bearing.

Having said this, however, you should also know that, generally speaking, people tend to be highly inaccurate at profiling. Don't be surprised if you did poorly on the exercise; the accuracy of your performance is not the point. The point of the exercise is to identify your own biases and assumptions, and then to understand how and when they steer you wrong. That way, when you have to make a snap decision, you can at least control for your personal preconceptions so that you don't mistakenly use them for corroboration. The ability to make correct decisions with limited data is important in both the clandestine *and* the corporate worlds.

BUILDING RAPPORT

The fourth and final skill set utilized by CIA officers as they work their way through the recruitment cycle is a constant effort to build rapport and trust with their target. This is just as straight-forward as it sounds. You want your target to take a risk on your behalf? It doesn't matter whether you are recruiting a spy to sell you government secrets or asking your boss to promote you ahead of your peers. In either case you need your target to trust and re-spect you.

Notice that I did not say that he or she has to *like* you. Building rapport does not mean that you need to become your target's new best friend. In fact, I would caution against it. No one chooses a brain surgeon based on likability, right? You aren't trying to estab-lish a friendship—you are trying to establish a mutually beneficial professional relationship.

Along these lines, now may be the appropriate moment in this book to take a step back and add a note of caution.

A LESSON IN HUMILITY

In the last chapter I mentioned that the typical first-day-of-work reaction for new CIA officers is disappointment. Fast-forward a year, after the same officers have undergone extensive and rigorous training at "the Farm," the CIA's notoriously tough training ground, and the most common trait you will find among the newly minted officers is now . . . arrogance. Don't worry—it's only temporary. It does, however, lead to a passing tendency to use the training too literally and too forcefully.

See, clandestine service trainees are kept in a bizarre bubble dur-ing their training, isolated from the real secret missions while they learn the skills that will make them successful and keep them safe when they embark upon their careers overseas. The training is in-tense, and both the failure and dropout rates are high. But for all of its intensity, the training consists of elaborate but ultimately fictional scenarios. Upon its completion, the trainees *all* end up with a brag sheet of successfully accomplished "missions." They have all successfully survived mock interrogations, learned how to detect staged surveillance, and carried large sums of fake money across fake borders. This make-believe success, plus a year of being told that they are the "elite," the "cream of the crop," and the "best of the best," tends to inflate the trainees' egos a bit.

At one point I held a position in which I supervised a number of newly trained officers. The officers were bright, eager, and most had already achieved career success in a variety of fields prior to joining the agency. After the grueling year of training, they were ready to conquer the world; they quite literally swaggered. Their cockiness reminded me of two things: first, of my own class of CIA novices when we finished our training; and second, of my fellow graduates from my Ivy League university, all of whom had been heavily courted by future employers and lavished with generous starting salaries and signing bonuses. So rather than being put off by their arrogance, I was amused. I knew that these new officers, just like the new college grads, would soon enough come face-to-face with the real world, and that humility would reign once again.

The new officers' cockiness was mostly demonstrated by their overemphasis on being "Charming"—with a capital C. They were all extended handshake, wide smile, and slightly overbearing eye contact; they laughed too loudly and spent too much time on warm-up small talk, rather than just getting down to business. They made a point to use my name frequently during our initial conversations, and several emphasized their points by reaching out and gently touching my arm, as if the physical contact would add gravity to what they were saying. Annoying, right? And we've all seen it—it is the stereotypical used-car salesman technique, with an added dash of self-help guru and a splash of pop psychology. It puts most of us on edge when someone with whom we are trying to do business becomes overly friendly in a forced and artificial manner.

In fact, this excessive dose of personality is so common within the CIA that there exists a frequently used comeback among peers in the clandestine service—"Don't try to 'case officer' me." In this context, the term "case officer" as a verb means to schmooze, to bullshit, or to aggressively manipulate. Don't do it! In the corporate world, this type of behavior will be interpreted by your clients as insincerity, by your management as overconfidence, by your peers as braggadocio, and by your subordinates as patronizing.

For this reason, rather than including an exercise to develop your ability to establish rapport, which is a highly personalized task anyway, I instead include a note of caution. Establish trust and rapport through natural and *gradually* progressive contact and actions. Seek out small opportunities to demonstrate your skills and your trustworthiness in a professional capacity. Bringing your client a latte at every meeting may endear you on a caffeine level, but it won't get you a contract extension. It is far better to slowly and surely build a track record of integrity, directness, and skill.

By skillfully targeting the person who can most effectively help you get ahead, using strategic elicitation to get the information that you need in order to be successful, and then methodically and patiently developing trust and rapport with your target, you will find yourself becoming indispensable in no time.

CHAPTER THREE

Business Counterintelligence

The hotel bar had been crowded with trade show attendees all evening, but it was getting late and only a few stragglers remained. A man in a disheveled suit was nearing the bottom of his glass when a woman sat down on the barstool next to his. She wearily hoisted a heavy canvas bag emblazoned with the trade show logo onto the empty seat on her other side. She glanced at the lone man's name tag briefly and then pointed to her own, indicating that they were both attending the same event. "So," she asked, "are you celebrating or drowning your sorrows? It seems like a pretty tough sell out there this year."

In fact, the man had been having terrible luck lately with sales, and with several strong drinks already in his system, he didn't mind telling the stranger in the business suit that he was getting fed up with his current line of work. When she told him that she knew of a possible job opening for someone with his background, the man perked up and shifted immediately into interview mode. Eager to impress the woman who might be able to help him get a more lucrative position, he bragged at great length about both his current position and his previous experience working as a technician in a government laboratory in his home country. He might have embellished his track record slightly, but the woman seemed impressed, and she insisted on buying the next few rounds of drinks.

The woman in the business suit was me. The man was a target I had been studying and watching from afar for quite some time. When I finally found him sitting in the bar without any of his colleagues or fellow countrymen, and with his tongue already loosened by a few drinks, I knew that I had a golden opportunity. In his heavy accent, the man told me everything I needed to know about his background, including some compromising details about the research being conducted in the highly classified laboratory where he used to work. For the price of a few drinks and the hint of a job opportunity, the conference attendee provided me with information of great value to the U.S. government.

Most of us would like to believe that we wouldn't be such easy prey. Before you scorn the man for being an easy target, though, put yourself in his situation. Imagine yourself constantly on the road, traveling from trade show to client site to corporate retreat and back again. You spend your days in airports and your nights in hotels that have all started to look the same. You live out of a suitcase and rarely see your friends or family. When a well-dressed stranger with whom you clearly have business in common strikes up a friendly, benign conversation, wouldn't you welcome the opportunity to chat? The man wasn't necessarily an easy target—he was just a typical lonely business traveler. I'm quite sure that he had no idea whatsoever that the information he was providing was compromising or valuable.

If you had been in his place, would you have recognized the situation for what it was? It's doubtful. And if not, how do you enhance your sense of personal and business counterintelligence? Read on! The purpose of this chapter is to teach you what you need to know in order to protect yourself and your organization in a competitive business climate in which private citizens are increasingly facing some of the same threats that CIA officers have been dealing with for years.

NEW REALITIES = NEW RULES

The key to business counterintelligence is to avoid ever falling victim to information thieves who may target you without your even knowing it. If you think that you can safely skip this section of the book because your job doesn't give you access to "secrets," think again, since the very definition—and value—of secret information is constantly changing.

When the Cold War ended, the prevailing currency of the spy game changed. State secrets were devalued by the new openness of glasnost and the improvement of diplomatic relations between former enemies. Within the private sector, on the other hand, the value of trade secrets skyrocketed as the concept of a worldwide economy grew, and technology made the world suddenly seem to become a much smaller place. The post–Cold War changes in the global political economy turned the spy world on its head. Suddenly there was less need for clandestine officers within the traditional political arenas, and more need for them in the business world. Spies, being an entrepreneurial bunch by nature, embraced the shift.

With these changes, however, the predictability of espionage decreased. Whereas it was once fairly obvious what the KGB was after, for example, and just how far they would go to get it, suddenly a whole new target set emerged. Traveling business executives began to suspect that someone had been in their hotel rooms while they were out. Sales reps at highly specialized trade shows suddenly became very popular, and found themselves on the receiving end of numerous invitations to socialize. Business travelers in certain parts of the world were surprised by late-night knocks on their hotel room doors from attractive, scantily clad women claiming an overwhelming desire to "practice English." Those who gave in to temptation often discovered their pockets a little lighter the next morning. Briefcases and laptops were stolen with alarming frequency. American engineers of Chinese heritage were approached by Chinese officials who made aggressive pitches for sensitive information focused on ethnic and cultural loyalty. Spy tactics had trickled into the business world, and many executives were caught unawares.

It didn't take long for the rules and parameters of espionage to change forever.

State secrets are no longer the goal of choice for entrepreneurial spies; the spy game has now shifted toward private industry. The reason is simple: money. In fact, the FBI now estimates that losses stemming from industrial espionage are in the billions of dollars annually. Billions! It's no surprise, considering just how many ways—both legal *and* illegal—there are to obtain sensitive data from a company. To name just a few:

- Public record searches
- Dumpster diving
- Electronic surveillance[*]
- Interviews with former employees
- Reverse engineering
- Computer network intrusions
- Soliciting information from unwitting employees at industry events
- Planting of "mole" employees within a company
- Press articles
- Analysis of a company's Web traffic
- Computer theft
- Regulatory rulings obtained via Freedom of Information Act (FOIA) requests
- Patent reviews
- Creating mirror Web sites or phishing portals from a company's Web site
- Identity theft
- Fake job applicants
- Analysis of employee travel patterns
- Information obtained from consultants or contractors eager to share "success stories"
- Theft by disgruntled employees
- Internet worms
- Data confiscated by foreign officials during overseas travel
- Hiring away of key employees

---

* Think that this is an extreme example that doesn't happen outside of Tom Clancy novels? So did members of Hewlett-Packard's board of directors before their phone records were obtained and scrutinized back in 2005. Even vice presidential candidate Sarah Palin's personal e-mail account was hacked in 2008. And new allegations of phone tapping perpetrated by British tabloid newspapers owned by Rupert Murdoch seemed to be coming out daily as I wrote this book. It happens!

From the mundane (data mining) to the sensational (blackmail), there are countless ways for your competitors to obtain information that you would rather not share, and then use it to their advantage. Business counterintelligence refers to efforts to identify and thwart such damaging corporate espionage.

Don't skip this chapter just because your job doesn't give you access to information that is considered sensitive in the traditional sense. Certainly, companies that work on top-secret government contracts have extensive safeguards in place, and typically employ in-house security experts (many of whom are former CIA or FBI officers) who provide rigorous counterintelligence training to employees with access to classified information. But just because the information that you deal with on a daily basis isn't classified by the U.S. government doesn't mean that it isn't of significant value to *someone*.

For example, employees in human resource functions have access to personal information about other employees, as well as advance knowledge of key personnel changes. Lawyers, accountants, and finance professionals possess sensitive client information; many government employees have access to regulatory information that would be of great value to the regulated parties; hospital workers are in control of highly personal medical information; software engineers have access to source codes; research and development scientists know what their company is coming out with next; administrative professionals know their boss's home address, travel, and meeting schedules (and in many cases, his or her vices); network administrators have access to all of a company's electronic data; the janitor has physical access to the building and the computers when no one else is around . . . the list is endless. *The possible leaks are endless.*

Before you start protesting any of the above examples by citing the various laws, statutes, rules of professional conduct, or ethical standards that *should* prevent any of these groups of people from divulging information, take a moment to consider the reality. Yes, it may be illegal, unfair, counterproductive, and just plain wrong, *but it happens.* Insider trading happens. Source code is leaked to overseas manufacturers who produce pirated versions. Tabloid magazines obtain and publish highly personal medical data about celebrities—including Britney Spears and Whitney Houston in two highly publicized cases. Films and music albums appear for sale overseas well in advance of their official release dates. Employees sell data, leak data, or even just accidentally leave laptops containing data in the back of a cab. It happens.

Like it or not, there is an enormous and powerful market for stolen information. People who make their living by dealing in black market data are shrewd, manipulative, and proficient at obtaining information from both complicit and unwitting sources.

Feeling paranoid yet? Pristine information security practices and judicious use of nondisclosure agreements can be very helpful in protecting your sensitive data, but legal and technical precautions can go only so far. Ultimately, there is no foolproof method to protect against the collection of human intelligence. Your best defense is an acute sense of awareness, and a practiced ability to sense a scam. And what better way to hone your senses than to know what it feels like to be on the *other* side.

COUNTERINTELLIGENCE EXERCISE

In order to know what it feels like to be unwittingly solicited for information, you need more experience in the fine art of strategic elicitation. This exercise brings more of a business focus to the new skill set that you practiced in the last chapter. If this exercise seems slightly repetitive, it is because the more times you go through the mental gymnastics associated with unobtrusive, successful elicitation, the better you will be at detecting someone else's efforts to pump you for information.

This exercise has two parts—one involving a stranger, and one involving a colleague. You'll see why later.

First, you'll need to find a target with whom you are *not* already acquainted. This exercise is best conducted using a captive audience; a fellow business traveler seated next to you on an airplane or train is ideal. Using the elicitation skills that you learned in chapter 2, your goal is to learn something specific about your target's future professional plans. Depending on his or her occupation, this could be a plan to switch employers, a hoped-for promotion, a pending retirement, or a specific professional accomplishment.

This goal is not overly intrusive or even outside of the bounds of a normal conversation with a fellow business professional, so it may seem fairly easy. However, there is an important lesson to be learned. The precept to focus on here is the concept of a multipronged line of elicitation. In order to achieve your goal, you will need to: first initiate contact and establish rapport, subsequently determine your target's profession, then direct your conversation toward your target's industry, then focus your conversation on your target's career, and finally elicit future professional plans.

So although it would not be uncommon for a casual chat between airplane-seat neighbors naturally to reveal the very information you are seeking in this exercise, the key learning point is to chain your questions in such a way that your elicitation appears to be nothing more than a logically flowing conversation.

Don't be surprised to find that when you have a specific goal and a finite amount of time to achieve it, you may be frustrated by veering, tangential topics or a conversation-dominating target. This happens to CIA officers all the time! Sometimes you may just want the answer to a simple technical question, but your target insists upon talking endlessly about problems with his mother-in-law. Try to strike a balance between maintaining control of the conversation and letting the discussion flow naturally.

Next, repeat the exercise with either a colleague or a business professional with whom you *are* already acquainted. Pick a target whom you know on a professional, but not a personal level. This time, seek information about either your target's future career plans or specific information about the future of one of his or her ongoing projects.

You will quickly discover that you can be far more direct in your elicitations with someone who is in your field, and with whom you already have a professional connection. You will undoubtedly achieve your goal far more rapidly than you did with your stranger target. This is only natural—in the second part of this exercise, you are dealing with someone who already knows you and your professional background. You have a built-in reason to elicit business-related information. Unlike in the first part of the exercise, you therefore don't have to spend time developing rapport and circuitously getting to your ultimate goal.

"So what?" you may be wondering about this exercise. Well, the effect of the trust and rapport afforded by a preexisting connection is well known to those people who make it their business to steal secrets. That's why in the scenario described in the opening of this chapter, I made it a point to carry my conference tote, to draw attention to my conference name tag, and to wear a business suit. These physical cues established an instant commonality between me and my target. We were at the same conference, which implied that we worked in the same industry, which meant that we could speak more openly with one another than with a perfect stranger. Had I approached my target at a random venue wearing a tourist's casual clothing and simply struck up a chance conversation, I would have had to work much harder to turn the conversation toward pro-

fessional matters, and my target would likely have considered my approach to be suspicious and unnatural.

COUNTERINTELLIGENCE SECURITY TIPS

Now that you have experience being the elicit*or* in various contexts, you are better prepared to recognize the warning signs that someone is trying to manipulate *you* into divulging information. Here are some steps that you can take to further protect yourself:

▶ **Travel with only as much data as you need for the trip.** Consider having a laptop computer dedicated to travel; this laptop should be kept free of personal data, saved passwords, or any other sensitive information. Take advantage of readily available technology to help protect your data, including biometric access devices, removable hard drives, encryption software, and data-wiping programs. You are far more likely to fall victim to theft while traveling, so plan ahead.

▶ **Be wary of public electronic venues.** If possible, avoid Internet cafés, hotel business center computers, and public Wi-Fi access points. If you don't control the security of the network that you are using, assume that it is compromised, and use it accordingly.

▶ **Shred!** This is basic, but important. Dumpster divers can't do anything with shredded documents.

▶ **Be aware of your public footprint.** Conduct due diligence on your own identity by searching the Internet and knowing what is available through public records. I recently helped a friend investigate his public footprint. Within just a few minutes of searching, I discovered where he worked as a teacher, his photo, that he was a coach for a sports team, and the schedule for the entire season's games, including locations. I also discovered postings on a gourmet food site in which he inquired about recommended restaurants for an upcoming international trip, including dates. Publicly available property records revealed his address, and the rather steep price that he had paid for his house. Had I been interested in robbing his expensive home, I would have a long list of dates and times when he was certain to be away.

▶ **Be wary of social networking sites, blogs, and Twitter.** They may be wonderful for keeping in touch with friends and family, but they should be used with the *assumption* that someone, somewhere is watching what you post with less than noble motives. No matter how much attention you pay to security settings when you set up your account profiles, understand that social networking tools were created to *share* data, not protect it.

▶ **Don't be lulled into a false sense of security by familiarity or professional qualifications.** Your cubicle neighbor may suddenly be much chattier than usual because he is competing with you for a promotion, just as the friendly person on the barstool next to yours at the convention may have an ulterior motive for asking so many questions.

▶ **Trust your instincts.** If your "spidey sense" tells you that something is awry, take action. Change the subject, divert and distract, or leave the room, as necessary. If your conversation partner doggedly pursues an uncomfortable line of questioning, he or she is either rude, oblivious, or eliciting. In each of those cases, you're well justified in ending the conversation.

► **Maintain firm boundaries.** It may seem tempting to share information in order to prove your knowledge during a job interview with a competing company, but a reputable interviewer should be more interested in learning about *you* than about your previous employer.

► **Save the party for later.** It can be tempting to use alcohol or sleep aids to help you grab a little rest during those dreadful red-eye flights, or when your internal clock refuses to catch up with multiple time zone changes. Be mindful, though, that alcohol can be a spy's best friend. I quite often plied my targets with drinks in order to impair their judgment and encourage booze-induced chattiness. You may think that you are in control as long as you aren't drunk and disorderly, but trust me—you are a far easier target even when you are just slightly under the influence.

In a world where information has a price, it pays to be vigilant. However, at the risk of contradicting myself, I would also caution you against paranoia. I know many CIA officers who are so protective of their clandestine status that they are reluctant to reveal even harmless personal details. Not only does this make it extremely difficult to have a normal conversation with them, but they also manage to stand out suspiciously because of their overly secretive demeanor.

Moreover, the reality is that business counterintelligence is generally of more concern at the organizational than the personal level. Other than the most senior executives, it is the rare private-sector individual who is targeted for reasons other than proximity and vulnerability (in other words, for being in the wrong place at the wrong time). Unless you have a particularly sensitive position or unique access to highly compartmentalized data, information thieves typically view you as interchangeable with any of your colleagues (just when you were feeling special!). *You* are only one of many different ways to get at data. As a result, even basic precautions and vigilant situational awareness can drastically reduce your chance of falling prey to scams. Just as a burglar will choose to skip the house with the barking dog in order to rob the less protected house next door, so will data thieves opt for the easiest target.

Nevertheless, a healthy sense of caution and fine-tuned observational skills can benefit anyone, in any position—whether the threat comes from organized industrial espionage or simply a co-worker who is trying to sabotage your chances of promotion. Business counterintelligence fundamentals are valuable tools whether you are flying first class to Shanghai or just riding the metro in from the suburbs.

ORGANIZATIONAL COUNTERINTELLIGENCE

Counterintelligence is a more difficult subject to tackle at the organizational than the personal level, for a variety of reasons.

First, at the organizational level an overemphasis on security and compartmentalization is counterproductive, and even detrimental. While an overly secretive individual will simply appear to be strangely reserved or standoffish, an organization with an overabundance of secrecy will fail to flourish. Can you imagine a company in which the senior management team is not allowed to share data, even with one another? Their information would be secure, but their ability to make informed decisions would be severely diminished.

Organizational security, by definition, restricts communication and collaboration. There are pros and cons to enforcing security, then. No matter how sensitive the industry, a certain level of transparency and communication within an organization is necessary in order to leverage intellectual capital, minimize redundancy, and to simply ensure that everyone has the information they need to get their jobs done. Balancing communication and security can be a difficult task. The CIA has struggled endlessly with the dueling requirements to both share and protect information; there exists a perennial internal battle in the intelligence community between analysts who need access to data in order to produce finished intelligence and the clandestine collectors who have to personally deal with the sometimes horrible repercussions of leaked information. There is no easy answer, and CIA officials have become accustomed to navigating the difficult and perpetually changing gray area between too much and not enough secrecy.

Organizational counterintelligence is also a difficult subject to tackle because good counterintelligence practices can be highly variable depending on the industry, the product, the nature of your competitive advantage, the critical skill sets, the relative strength of the competition, the geographic location, and even the economy. Nevertheless, the need to use good business counterintelligence practices applies whether you are a one-person business in which you, the sole employee, work at home in your pajamas, or a multinational corporation with a global presence. If you have even a single competitor—whether that competitor is a co-worker or a rival company—you have a valid reason to safeguard your competitive advantage.

Most companies fall into the trap of believing that adequate physical and IT security will suffice to protect their business from industrial espionage or sabotage. But if you rely on door locks and firewalls, you are still leaving yourself open to each and every person who has a key and a password, and your business will only be as secure as your most unethical/disgruntled/sloppy/debt-ridden (pick your vulnerability) employee. Take it from someone who spent years stealing secrets from people—security and counterintelligence plans that ignore human frailties are incomplete at best. Consider the following hard lesson in counterintelligence:

For several long decades, the CIA believed that it had a thriving Cuban intelligence collection program. Most of the program's assets were disgruntled Cuban officials who in many cases had simply walked into a U.S. embassy to volunteer their services and their data. Claiming to be motivated by frustration with or mistreatment from Fidel Castro's regime, the sources provided detailed information that could be corroborated by the reporting of separate, unrelated assets. This corroboration, plus the fact that most of the Cuban assets passed polygraphs, was taken as proof that these spies were the real deal. Because the information provided by the Cuban sources was used to make critical foreign policy and military decisions, intelligence consumers and policy makers pushed for more and more detail. Over time, the assets were tasked with increasingly sensitive collection requirements, and were trained in clandestine communications and operations.

Then the worst-case scenario happened. In the late 1980s, the CIA's clandestine Cuba program was blown apart by stunning revelations from several high-level Cuban intelligence officials who defected to the United States. These "real" defectors revealed that most, if not all, of the CIA's Cuban assets were in fact double agents. Not only had they been providing false information, but they had been reporting back to the Cuban government all of the sensitive taskings and training provided by their CIA handlers. As a result, Cuban

intelligence officials gained a clear picture of exactly
what the United States did and did not know, and perhaps even more damaging, Cuba learned the methods
and technology used by the CIA, along with the identi-
ties of many of our undercover officers. In the wake of
the defectors' revelations, Castro gloated publicly about
the long-term deception, and Cuban television aired hu-
miliating footage of CIA officers who had been secretly
videotaped while engaged in what they believed to be
clandestine activities.

The Cuban double-agent fiasco is an embarrassing chapter in
CIA history, and a great deal of effort has gone into trying to understand what went wrong. Myriad after-action reports and investigations placed blame on everyone from the polygraphers who failed to
catch signs of deception to the case officers who failed to spot the
surveillance tracking their every move to the policy makers who put
pressure on the CIA to aggressively collect information, even in the
face of mounting discrepancies and warning signs. The bottom line
is that the Cuban double agents were able to circumvent both technical security measures (they had received extensive training that
enabled them to pass polygraph exams) and physical ones (surveillance detection proved useless against the Cuban intelligence service's scrutiny).

So how difficult would it be to pose a similar threat to private
industry? Not very difficult at all, unfortunately. Consider the following, parallel example:

Nathan, the founder of a medium-sized construction
firm, considered himself to be security-conscious and
technology-savvy. After falling victim to equipment
theft on several work sites early in his career, he made

it a point to meticulously secure both his office and his job sites, and his employees were required to complete a security checklist at the end of each business day to make sure nothing fell through the cracks. In addition, he contracted with an IT consultant who meticulously kept his company's computers up to date with security software. His employees did not know that he periodically monitored their Internet use or read their e-mails; he considered it to be management's prerogative to know what his employees were doing during working hours. Nathan considered himself to be an excellent judge of character, and even though his company's head count had increased greatly over the years, he still insisted on personally interviewing each and every job candidate. On more than one occasion, he had rejected an applicant simply because of a gut feeling that the person was dishonest.

Nathan had done well in a difficult market, but in 2008 he started losing bids with disturbing frequency, and by midyear he was forced to lay off several project managers and his office manager. Out of a sense of fairness, he implemented a "last in, first out" policy, laying off the most junior employees first. Shortly after the layoffs his luck seemed to turn around, and he won the bids for several large jobs in a row. Happily, he felt confident enough about the future of the company to reach out to the recently laid-off employees to offer them their jobs back. Because he seemed to have misplaced his Rolodex in the chaos of the down period, he did a quick Internet search to find the contact information for his former office manager, who had been with the company for less than a year before he had to let her go.

Nathan's Internet search revealed much more than the office manager's contact information, however. He was horrified to discover that his office manager, whom he had believed to be a diligent and efficient addition to his company, was in fact the daughter-in-law of one of his biggest competitors, a man who had a reputation for playing dirty. Staring at the recent wedding announcement, which was accompanied by a smiling picture of his former office manager and her new in-laws, Nathan realized that his company's dry spell had been due to much more than bad luck. The office manager had helped him compile and finalize all of his sealed bids— for the same jobs that he had lost to the very man who was smiling proudly in the wedding photo. It was painfully clear that his trusted assistant had been leaking information that allowed her father-in-law's company to undercut Nathan's bids. To add insult to injury, it suddenly occurred to Nathan that his Rolodex, which had contained years of accumulated industry contacts, had gone missing on the office manager's last day.

After a discouraging consultation with his lawyer, Nathan decided not to pursue the matter. Both his bottom line and his pride had been wounded, and he was haunted by the feeling that his competitors were laughing at him for being such a fool. Deeply shaken by the experience, he knew that although he would recover financially, he would never again be able to trust his ability to judge a person's character.

In both examples, the "double agents" were able to inflict great damage to their targets in large part because the respective organizations relied too heavily on flawed and incomplete screening systems. Once the double agents made it past the initial screening, they were considered trustworthy, and were able to easily wreak havoc from within.

Worth noting, too, is that in both cases the damage was inflicted by relatively unsophisticated means against organizations that otherwise paid close attention to technical and physical security. In the first example, many of the Cuban double agents literally walked into U.S. embassies and volunteered their services. In the second example, the perpetrator easily obtained an entry-level job and simply reported basic data back to the competition. Why bother hacking into computers, tapping phones, or taking the risk of a physical intrusion if you can just send an agent right through your target's front door? And yet many companies that spend huge amounts of money on computer and physical security continue to ignore the more basic risks from within.

In both examples, the screening processes failed to protect. Cuban double agents were able to deceive polygraphers and to corroborate one another's information, and the office manager appeared to be trustworthy and competent. Yet while effective screening processes, which will be addressed in detail in the next chapter, are extremely important, they are only a small part of good counterintelligence practices. In fact, to most thoroughly protect your organization against corporate espionage or sabotage, you need to *assume* that there is already a threat lurking within.

Assuming the existence of an internal threat may sound paranoid and extreme, particularly for those of you who trust and value your employees and co-workers. And if you start to treat your fellow professionals as potential spies, you likely won't have a loyal team around you for long. Therefore, it is important that you don't adopt the assumption of an internal threat as a *mind-set,* but rather that you use it as a factual hypothesis with which to drive your security and counterintelligence practices.

Here is how to use the assumption of an internal threat in a positive, proactive manner:

1. Make sure that your network has deep roots. Too many business executives rise through the corporate ranks without ever looking back. After all, who doesn't want to leave the lean years behind? But in surrounding yourself with a network made exclusively of your ever more senior peers, you lose out on a critical information source. Who do you think is more difficult for a CIA officer to recruit: a senior diplomat who comes from a wealthy family, or the man who works in the embassy's mailroom, hasn't received a promotion in over a decade, and is struggling to support his ailing parents and three young children? The mail clerk has far more obvious vulnerabilities, and with his access to the very same sensitive documents as the diplomat, he would be a prime target for recruitment.

This does *not* mean that you should treat lower-level employees as more likely to be potential spies. Rather, it means that you should stay connected with people at all levels in your organization. Maintaining a reputation for being open and responsive to communication from all sources will ensure that whoever notices something amiss will bring that information to you right away. Besides, most corporate espionage attempts begin with low-level probes. You could be tipped off to early warning signs by the customer service representative who notices a string of strange inquiries, by the night janitor who sees men going through the Dumpsters outside your building, or by the HR assistant who notices that quite a few of your employees are quitting to go work for a particular competitor. If your subordinates don't have confidence that you will be receptive to their observations, they won't bring them to you, and you will miss out on valuable opportunities to catch threats early.

2. Respect data *and* intuition. CIA officers funnel their collected intelligence to analysts who are experts in using the aggregate data to observe trends, detect subtle shifts, and track changes. Unless your organization has its own dedicated competitive intelligence function, *you* will need to be your own trend analyst.

Most companies are scrupulous about analyzing financial data and trends, but ignore other information that can have just as much impact on the bottom line. Your best allies in trend spotting are those individuals in your organization who have the most pervasive contact with your employees and your customers: typically HR, sales, and customer service.

Important trends to watch will vary from industry to industry. However, from a basic counterintelligence standpoint, any company, large or small, should be mindful of changes to the following:

- Where are your former employees going to work?
- Which employees (e.g., from which department, division, branch, or skill set) are leaving?
- Where are your new hires coming from?
- What is the public saying about your company?
- Who is getting your lost clients/customers?
- How quickly are your competitors matching your changes and improvements?

Shifts in the aggregate responses to these questions can tell you whether someone is siphoning off your talent, planting employees, poisoning your reputation, or stealing company secrets. Many companies seek to answer the questions above by using employee exit questionnaires and formal customer satisfaction surveys. While these forms of data collection do have value, I would argue that they are insufficient. For one thing, there will always be a response bias. In the case of employee exit questionnaires, let's be honest. Few of us fill them out truthfully. Mindful of the need to leave on a good note (if nothing else because of the possible need for future job references), many employees who have legitimate gripes refrain from documenting the real reasons for their departure. Saying that you are "leaving for a shorter commute" is far less controversial than admitting "my new employer offered me a bonus for every client I bring with me," even if the latter is true.

Customer satisfaction surveys also have a response bias, since only your most and least satisfied customers will be inclined to take the time to answer the questions. Moreover—let's be honest again here—they can be just plain annoying. We're all inundated by calls, e-mails, and letters asking us to "answer a few questions" about our recent experiences with everything from small online purchases to medical appointments. I certainly appreciate the importance of this data collection, but as a busy consumer, I for one simply ignore most of these requests.

There are many consulting and research firms that, for a steep price, will administer and analyze your data; some of them claim to be able to eliminate the response bias with sophisticated statistical analysis. Even so, by the time a trend becomes quantifiable and the data is then collected, compiled, analyzed, and reported . . . you've lost valuable time.

Instead, as I mentioned in chapter 1, you need to develop an *instinctive* ability to spot threatening trends. The ability to sniff out a threat by trend spotting comes from an in-depth knowledge of your industry, information from your organization's front lines, and constant attention to subtle changes. With these factors, *you* can be a far better trend spotter, and therefore a far better barometer of looming counterintelligence threats, than any questionnaire.

3. Listen to your detractors. For CIA officers, nothing is as important as obtaining secret information from the groups and nations most likely to cause harm to our country. Information about a terrorist network's plans and capabilities, or a hostile nation's military preparedness, is of far more value than, say, inside information about a friendly nation's political maneuverings. In fact, officers posted to some of the cushier assignments in Western Europe are often derided as being "on the cocktail circuit," instead of spending their time in the hardship posts. Generally speaking, the more critical and potentially damaging the information, the closer attention the intelligence community will pay, and the more accolades the CIA officer will receive for obtaining it. In a strange way, then, the more negative the information reported by a spy, the better it is for his or her career.

It is just the opposite in the business world, where no one wants to be the bearer of bad news, and no one likes to hear from detractors. One reason for this is the compensation goal bias. Most compensation systems reward the achievement of goals, and most goals are structured as positive accomplishments (e.g., a bonus will be paid out for achieving X goal, or for meeting Y timeline). Obviously, people are much more inclined to draw attention to data that gets them closer to their goals, and therefore closer to their bonus payouts. As a result, achievements are reported and celebrated, but problems remain unspoken. This compensation goal bias increases exponentially the higher you go in an organization, particularly as base pay becomes a smaller and smaller component of an overall compensation package. Unlike CIA officers, then, CEOs get paid to achieve positive results, not to seek out bad news—as well they should. However, when you ignore detractors you are also ignoring potential threats.

Listening to detractors goes hand in hand with trend spotting. One unhappy client can be chalked up as the price of doing business. A series of clients with similar complaints is a threatening trend that needs to be addressed. The same holds true within organizations: mass resignations, diminishing morale, rapid turnover within senior positions, or any other negative trend warrants careful attention, even when there is no immediately apparent effect on the bottom line. Since I've already expressed my concerns about relying exclusively on surveys, here are a few tips for other ways to effectively monitor dissenting opinions, both internally and externally:

▶ **Know who is leaving unhappy.** A relatively senior member of the management team should conduct exit interviews for all departing employees. The CIA is very wary of employees leaving on an unhappy note—a disgruntled individual leaving with information from years' worth of access to top-secret data can be a dangerous thing indeed. Disgruntled private-sector employees should also be a thing to avoid. Exit interviews, if conducted in a consistent, supportive, confidential manner, can yield far more accurate information than a written survey. The data may yield one of two things: legitimate complaints about the employer that should be addressed, or invalid gripes from individuals who simply didn't fit in the organization. Even in the case of an employee who never should have been hired, though, it is better to know where you stand before the former employee walks out the door for the last time, for several reasons. First, recognizing hiring errors can help improve your organization's recruitment process. In addition, knowing who is leaving unhappy can also identify possible threats to the organization. Disgruntled former employees can provide information to your competitors, damage your reputation, or even sabotage ongoing projects. Most departing employees will do no such thing, of course, but it is in everyone's best interest for your employees to walk out the door without bitterness or anger. The CIA has an extensive exit process, consisting of multiple interviews for departing officers to ensure that they have a full understanding of both the reasons and, perhaps more important, the risks associated with each and every employee departure.

▶ **Assess the "mood."** In addition to collecting quantifiable data about customer complaints, develop a sense for the customer service atmosphere. Does this sound a bit like hocus-pocus? It's not. Just picture the difference between two long queues of people: one consists of the people who lined up many hours in advance just to be one of the first to buy the latest-generation iPhone; the other consists of travelers waiting at the airline customer service counter after learning that their flight has been canceled. You don't have to be a terribly perceptive person to observe that the people in the first line are eager and excited, while the people in the second line are weary and irate. *That's* the mood of your customer base.

Consumer mood can, of course, be influenced by many factors that are not within your company's sphere of control. But just as a CIA officer's recruitment strategy is influenced by a target's preexisting perception of the United States and its representatives, so should business strategy be influenced by its customers' perceptions—whether those perceptions are shaped by internal or external variables.

▶ **Understand your company's public footprint.** There are online consumer reviews for just about every product and service. Know what reviewers are saying about your organization—both on the major review sites for your industry and on individual blogs and comments. Know what comes up when people plug your organization's name into the various popular search engines. Set up Google Alerts so that you know when your organization is being written about online. You may or may not agree with what you find, but you should always be aware. The CIA requires all employees—current and former—to submit drafts of books, articles, or speeches for approval prior to public release. Obviously, private organizations cannot enforce this type of requirement, but just because you can't censor critics doesn't mean that you should ignore what they are saying about you in the public domain.

4. Acknowledge your weaknesses and vulnerabilities—even those you've worked hard to cultivate. To their credit, most business leaders are focused on building strengths and eliminating or minimizing weaknesses. But let's get a little bit Zen here: it is possible for your organization's greatest strength to also be one of its greatest vulnerabilities. This is true on several levels.

For starters, the tougher the market and the greater the disparity between competitors, the more vulnerable the top player is to espionage. In the intelligence world, this plays out in the form of dramatically increased efforts to spy on the United States during times of economic crisis or military conflict. In the private sector, it plays out in the form of the hungriest underdog competitors being willing to be more aggressive, and sometimes more unscrupulous, during market downturns. If your organization is thriving in a tough field, be proud, but watch your back.

Strength as vulnerability is also true on a more specific level: your competitive advantage is what your foes most want to steal.

In the clandestine world, this can be seen most clearly in the counterproliferation arena of the spy game. Because the acquisition of nuclear capabilities would give certain hostile nations an unacceptable military advantage, CIA officers labor endlessly to identify, thwart, and destroy burgeoning nuclear programs among rogue nations. The stronger the developing program, the more resources that are thrown against it. Therefore, a strong nuclear development program can be more of a vulnerability than an asset for hostile nations—it tends to invite much more unwanted attention from the CIA than any nation wants to deal with.

In the private sector, the concept of strength as vulnerability means that your organization's competitive advantage also serves as a big flashing target for your competitors. Is your competitive advantage a stellar reputation for customer care? Then you are all the more vulnerable to negative publicity orchestrated by your rivals. Is your competitive advantage your ability to attract the top talent in your industry? Then the headhunters employed by your competitors will seek out your employees first. Is innovation your competitive advantage? Then your foes will try to learn and copy your plans. Is your low price point your greatest strength? Then your competitors can try to steal, corrupt, or duplicate your supplier and distribution networks.

In the same vein, you also need to understand your *competitors'* weaknesses in order to understand your own vulnerabilities. Your competitors will naturally seek what they lack, and if your organization has it in abundance, you are vulnerable. For example, if your competition lacks an effective marketing strategy, treat your marketing team well, since they are coveted experts vulnerable to recruitment efforts.

Use your assessment of your organization's vulnerabilities to strategically protect your competitive advantage against all potential threats.

RED CELLS

Within the walls of the CIA is a special room—a safe haven for paranoia, delusional thinking, conspiracy theories, outlandish statements, and extremism of all sorts. Here meets the so-called Red Cell team, whose purpose is to concoct elaborate and often implausible disaster and attack scenarios and then determine how our country's security defenses would react. If an idea is ever criticized as too preposterous, participants are reminded that an attack involving flying airplanes into skyscrapers also once sounded ridiculous.

The purpose of a Red Cell is to imagine the unlikely, predict the unpredictable, and then hypothetically test possible responses and outcomes. Lest you think that this might be an ineffective endeavor in the private sector, consider the "unforeseeable" toll that the subprime mortgage crisis has taken on the financial industry, and the commensurate effects on nearly every sector out there. As I write this, the very future of a number of industry titans in sectors ranging from aerospace to retail is uncertain. Not long ago, the executives of these companies likely thought the possibility of imminent collapse was absurd.

But what if they had at least considered the possibility? What if they had identified the early indicators of looming failure and acted sooner? No one can predict the future, but adopting the CIA's Red Cell techniques can at least help organizations (or individuals, for that matter) articulate and plan for scenarios that would otherwise catch them unawares and unprepared.

Red Cell Exercise

For this exercise, I want you to serve as your own Red Cell. You can answer as either an individual or as an organization. Let's begin:

- First, come up with two competitors. They can either be real-life competitors or they can be theoretical. One competitor should be legitimate and conventional; assume that this party will operate within the constraints of the law. The second competitor should be as devious and unethical as they come; assume that this party will use any means necessary to get what it wants.
- Now list your strengths or competitive advantages. What

makes you or your organization a rival, and therefore a target?

- Next, list your weaknesses and vulnerabilities.

- Finally, come up with a list of all of the different ways that each competitor could (a) exploit your vulnerabilities, and (b) steal or destroy your competitive advantage.

In order to make the most out of this task, you need to strike a balance somewhere between letting your imagination run completely amok and conventional, "in the box" thinking. This should be an exercise in structured paranoia, if you will. No fair, then, listing "zombie apocalypse" as one of the threats against your organization. Do, however, get creative and try to imagine the unimaginable.

Once you have completed your lists, focus on the differences between the possible threats from the ethical versus the dirty competitor. Are there substantial differences? Or can your vulnerabilities be just as readily exploited by conventional, legal methods?

Can you realistically protect yourself or your organization from the possible threats posed by the two competitors? How? Or will you just have to accept the risks as the price of doing business?

Using Red Cell techniques to identify and analyze even the wildest of possible threats is useful both for planning purposes and to further develop your ability to intuitively sense threats and opportunities. Besides, as William S. Burroughs once wrote, "Sometimes paranoia's just having all the facts."

FINDING SECURITY IN AN INSECURE WORLD

Now that you know your vulnerabilities and how to identify attempts to exploit them, you are well on your way to being secure. Surprised that it is this simple? The world of industrial counterintelligence is full of misconceptions, one of which is that economic espionage can only be countered by expensive and elaborate means worthy of Hollywood. In reality, business counterintelligence practices are usually not complicated or cloak-and-dagger; they don't involve secret passwords or late-night meetings in dark alleyways. Instead, business counterintelligence is primarily about vigilance, good security practices, and checks and balances.

It is another common fallacy that counterintelligence is important only to businesses whose intellectual property worth exceeds their brick-and-mortar worth. Business counterintelligence does not just address information theft. It also deals with employee or skill set theft, customer theft, and product piracy.

Similarly, many believe that only the top executives in major companies are at risk for becoming victims of corporate espionage, or that only companies dealing in secretive or classified industries are vulnerable. To the contrary, even the smallest companies in any industry can be victims.

Nevertheless, there *are* factors that heighten your organization's CI risk:

- Frequent foreign travel by employees
- Foreign subsidies or partnerships
- Extensive use of subcontractors
- Highly competitive industries with limited, high-stakes opportunities
- IT vulnerabilities
- Interaction with foreign governments for regulatory or compliance purposes
- Disgruntled employees (either current or former)
- Manufacture of frequently pirated goods
- Highly specialized skill set required of employees, combined with an overall shortage of qualified people

- Executives with exploitable vulnerabilities such as alcoholism or drug use, or behaviors that make them susceptible to blackmail

As you can see, some of these risks are controllable, and some are not—this is the very nature of business counterintelligence. No matter what your position, your industry, or your competition, there is always the possibility of industrial espionage or sabotage. The risks can be minimized, however, with scrupulous attention to proper counterintelligence practices. To be aware and secure is to be protected.

Part Two

INTERNAL APPLICATIONS

CHAPTER FOUR

Creating Your Team:
Recruitment and Organizational Strategies from the CIA

Now that I've filled your head with visions of sabotage and planted moles, and probably made you generally suspicious of human contact, would it seem strange for me to begin this chapter by parroting the oft-repeated mantra that "your employees are your greatest asset"? We've already established, after all, that they are your company's greatest vulnerability.

And yet I can't help but agree that organizations rise and fall with the talent found within.

Your employees are your greatest strength *and* your greatest weakness. This duality is simply human nature.

The recruitment strategy used by the CIA not only acknowledges this duality—it actually embraces it. After all, the CIA has to narrow down its many thousands of applicants to the small group of people who are (a) squeaky clean enough to pass a brutally thorough background check, (b) mentally sound enough to pass batteries of psychological tests, (c) personable and intelligent enough to make it through numerous interviews with former case officers who can be very tough judges of character, and (d) healthy enough to pass comprehensive physical screenings. From this group of virtuous, smart, sane, healthy, and likable individuals, CIA recruiters then need to cull out those applicants who are *also* willing to lie, cheat, and steal for their country. In other words, the recruiters have to find those people who are willing and able to skillfully engage in dodgy behavior, but who have a strong enough moral code that they have not yet done so. (I have heard the ideal candidate described as a "Boy Scout with a latent dark side.") With these paradoxical requirements, I don't envy CIA recruiters their jobs.

The successful candidates represent a very, very small subset of the overall applicants, let alone the American population. Low government starting salaries then discourage some of those who make it through the screening process and receive job offers; it is quite common for new hires to take significant pay cuts in order to become CIA officers. Other offer recipients decide that they don't like the idea of lying to friends and family—a necessary evil for undercover work. The group of those who are chosen and who then accept the job offer is subsequently diminished even further by a grueling yearlong training program. Many opt out once they see the realities of the undercover life, and many are asked to leave as it becomes clear that they aren't cut out for the rigors of the top-secret world.

The CIA's actual recruitment and training budget is classified, but it is no secret that it is very, *very* expensive. No other organization in the world could possibly justify the cost per hire accrued by the agency.

So, given the fact that no one in their right mind wants to emulate the CIA's recruitment costs, nor to employ the teams of psychologists and polygraphers, accept the staggering attrition rate, or take up to several years to complete a single hire—what can you possibly borrow from the CIA's recruitment process?

Plenty.

ORGANIZATIONAL PROFILING

It's no surprise that the CIA, with its staff psychologists, expert profilers, and large cadre of experienced officers, has a very specific idea about what type of person has the potential to become a good case officer. They have determined, through years of trial and error, as well as empirical research, which skills, personality traits, previous experiences, and even beliefs serve as measurable indicators that an applicant not only has the ability to perform the basic work of a case officer, but also the fortitude to withstand the emotional pressures of the undercover lifestyle. For a job as demanding, important, and sometimes dangerous as that of an undercover CIA officer, it is critical that the hiring decisions be as informed and accurate as humanly possible. The average hiring decisions within *your* organization may not have quite as much at stake, but that doesn't mean that you can't develop equally rigorous standards in order to build a better team.

Whether you are hiring a new employee, choosing who to promote from within, or simply selecting someone for a temporary assignment, you need to have a firm grasp of the critical skill set required for the position as well as a profile of the ideal person for the job. This may sound obvious, but I have observed organizations making the following three mistakes, over and over again:

I. Hiring by gut. I warned you in chapter 2 that people who consider themselves to be superior judges of character are often simply the most overconfident in their assumptions and biases. And yet it is disturbingly common for otherwise intelligent, detail-oriented, experienced professionals to base their hiring decisions on their "gut feelings" about a candidate.

Proponents of intuition-based hiring argue that they know whom they like, whom they can get along with, and who they can work alongside. One hiring manager at a prestigious consulting firm told me that by the time candidates walked through his door for an interview, their educational credentials and past work experience had already been prescreened by the HR recruiting team. He therefore felt free to assume that all of the candidates were thoroughly qualified in terms of skills, and thus that he should be making the final decision based primarily on personality.

This is *almost* a convincing argument. After all, if you know that two people are qualified to do the job, why not hire the candidate who seems more likable?

There are several flaws in this logic, however. First, even if you are scrupulously applying your strategic elicitation and observational skills from chapter 2, a job interview is a highly artificial environment and is not conducive to making accurate personality assessments. Job candidates are wearing their best suits, using their firmest handshakes, and spitting out their best (i.e., most rehearsed) answers to your questions. The problem drinkers are abstaining during the interview lunch, the sexual harassers are keeping their eyes front and center, and the liars are spinning their most convincing tales. Prescreening may mean that everyone who walks into your office for an interview is *smart*, but there are plenty of smart liars, thieves, and jerks in the world.

Another problem with hiring by your gut is the problem of "like attracts like." This is a concept that has been borrowed and distorted a bit by some recent popular pop psychology books. Don't worry—I'm not getting mystical on you here. For my purposes, it refers to the tendency to be drawn to those people with whom you share the most in common. It's only natural to feel more comfortable conversing with someone with whom you share an alma mater, a mutual friend, or a favorite pastime. The problem with this is that the tendency to favor those who are the most like you can result in a one-dimensional, homogeneous workforce (not to mention a major Equal Employment Opportunity problem).

When interviewing, keep in mind that you don't need to *like* your employees. You should respect and trust them, and be able to work side by side without conflict or animosity. Friendship in the workplace, however, should be a happy coincidence—*not* an employment requirement. Let your gut guide you if you think that there is something amiss during a job interview, but base your hiring decisions on facts instead of intuition.

2. Vague parameters. The second mistake that I see companies making repeatedly is the creation of vague, flowery hiring parameters. A number of years ago it became de rigueur to craft mission and value statements, and many companies created subsets of these statements for their hiring practices. These value statements appear prominently on corporate Web sites and in glossy recruiting brochures, and are often quoted in vacancy announcements.

I did a quick random Internet search of the recruitment Web sites of various large employers, and found that they were soliciting job seekers who demonstrated attributes such as the following: "best-in-class capabilities," "energy and enthusiasm," "active collaboration," "boundless determination," and "inclusive style." And appearing most frequently on the list of desired attributes? Passion. Employer after employer emphasized passion for various things, big and small. In my quick search, I found employers seeking "passion for" each of the following: innovation, people, technology, customer service, helping, excellence, continuous improvement, travel, fitness, design, banking, fashion, food, botany, excellence, learning, discovery, putting clients first, payroll, detail, drivetrains, online ad targeting, and "encouraging the use of primary materials" (this one was for a library job). Winning the prize for most generic passion statement was the stated desire for "passion for the job"—a phrase that I found over and over again.

From a marketing standpoint, listing these fuzzy qualities may be appropriate, but from a functional, internal standpoint, these value statements are utterly useless—particularly when they are used in lieu of more specific but less flashy lists of critical requirements against which to measure candidates.

Now consider the verbiage found on the CIA's public Web site. Clandestine service job seekers are advised the following:

[Officers] deal with fast-moving, ambiguous, and unstructured situations by combining their "people and street smarts" with subject matter expertise and a knowledge of foreign languages, areas, and cultures. . . . Operations Officers are given great amounts of responsibility and trust early in their careers. While they work in teams, they often need to "think on their feet," using common sense and flexibility to make quick decisions on their own. [They] have demanding responsibilities, often requiring them to work long, irregular hours so it is essential that they be physically and psychologically fit, energetic, and able to cope with stress. They must know themselves very well and a sense of humor is also a plus.

It's an ambitious job description, but it's a little more specific than "passion for the job," isn't it? And internally, you'd better believe that the applicant requirements are *far* more specific.

The tendency to use vague verbiage, however, is just a symptom of a bigger issue. The actual problem is that many employers utilize lofty and unrealistic parameters (Passion for payroll? Really?) instead of identifying the truly critical skill sets and articulating exactly what type of candidate is most likely to succeed in a given position, within a given organizational context.

Take the time to create a specific, actionable profile of your ideal new hire. Doing so will save you time in the long run, as it helps narrow down a large pool of candidates, and it will help ensure that your vision for the future of your organization is realized a step further with the entrance of each new employee.

3. Reinventing the wheel. On the opposite side of the spectrum from those organizations with poetic but ultimately useless hiring values statements are the employers who are so literal in their individual hiring practices that they never end up with any kind of a cohesive plan for growing their organizations into something better than the sum of the parts. Critical skill requirements are thought of in terms of specific degrees, exact minimum numbers of years of experience, and certifications necessary to complete the immediate task at hand. As such, the hiring goals are written on a very specific, case-by-case basis, and the organization's talent growth strategy is reinvented with each and every job opening. Each new hire is "ideal" only for the specific position and the specific hiring manager—not necessarily for the organization.

Somewhere between the fluff and the literal exists a recruitment strategy that can attract and select candidates who not only feel right on an interpersonal level, but who can also *measurably* demonstrate the skills critical for the immediate job, the next job in the succession model, and the organization as a whole. It may be a challenging task, but if the CIA can identify and hire "Boy Scouts with a latent dark side," your organization can surely identify the indicators of a talented, pleasant professional with the skill set and temperament for the job *and* for the organization.

EFFECTIVE SCREENING

The CIA's screening process is without doubt one of the most rigorous selection procedures in existence. The psychological tests, live scenario exercises, physical exams, confrontational interviews, and intrusive background investigations are topped off with the controversial and nerve-racking polygraph exam. And yet this screening is not used just to keep inappropriate applicants *out;* it is also used to help keep people *in.*

CIA recruiters make no secret of the rigors of the job. Even the online description for a case officer, quoted earlier in this chapter, makes full disclosure that the job is physically and psychologically demanding and requires long, irregular hours. These negative aspects are not disclosed for compassionate reasons; instead, CIA recruiters want to avoid going through the expense of hiring and training new officers, only to have them quit at the end of their training once they realize what the job actually entails.

Utilizing this type of disclosure does not mean that your job ads need to literally spell out all of the negatives. ("Seeking applicants for tedious clerical work for verbally abusive boss in a windowless office. Must be passionate about the job.") It does, however, mean that you need to understand and acknowledge that no job is perfect. The "best" (on paper) applicant you interview may also be the most likely to quit after two weeks if the job and the organization don't live up to the expectations that you as the employer have inaccurately conveyed. You would do better to assess candidates not only for how well they can meet the requirements, but also for how they might fare in the toughest circumstances that they are likely to face.

In general, of course, screening is used more often for the purpose of keeping unqualified applicants *out.* The CIA's screening methods may be a bit extreme, but any organization can borrow from its methods in order to narrow down the candidate pool to the best and the brightest. To do so, you'll need to draw on some of the skills that you practiced in chapter 2. Corroboration, in particular, is critical to effective screening.

1. Corroborate the facts. I am continually surprised by how many employers fail to verify résumé entries. At a minimum, you need to confirm previous employment and education; *any* false claim should instantly rule out a candidate.

Unfortunately, checking the references given by the applicant can be of minimal use, because the references have been preselected as those most likely to say positive things about the job candidate. No one uses as a reference the boss who fired them two weeks ago for incompetence! To combat this problem, CIA background investigators not only contact the references given by applicants, but they also ask *those* references for the names of additional contacts. They continue to branch out to additional references other than those originally supplied until they are satisfied. You can replicate this by maintaining a deep network within your industry and tapping into your contacts when you need to hear the *real* story. Within the clandestine service, this is often referred to as getting the "hall file"—as in the employee details discussed only in hushed tones in the hallway, rather than those found inside the formal personnel file. A candidate's "hall file" can be excellent or it can be grim; either way, the details are a very useful supplement to what you are likely to learn if you only take a cursory glance at a candidate's résumé.

2. Corroborate the skills. Don't take an applicant's word for skills and strengths; ask him or her for specific, concrete examples. Your top candidate claims to be a good writer? Ask for samples. She claims to be an effective manager? Ask for an example of how she dealt with a problem employee. He claims to be proficient in real estate law? Ask him a challenging legal question that he *should* be able to answer. She claims to have excellent customer service skills?

Role-play a scenario with her in which you portray a difficult customer, and see how she responds.

Developing an interview that can elicit and corroborate critical skills has the added advantage of allowing you to tap into a wider array of potential applicants. If you are relying exclusively on reading the right words on a résumé and hearing the right prememorized buzzwords during an interview, you may be missing out on better candidates who have a less traditional job history. By structuring your interview to elicit specific examples of critical skills, you free yourself from the tyranny of previous job titles. The lazy hiring manager only extends offers for an account executive position to those candidates with the requisite number of years in identically titled jobs. Managers with more confidence in their ability to elicit and corroborate the ideal skills for that position can seek potentially better candidates from outside of the traditional but often stale talent pool.

As an example, the CIA has recently started relaxing its strict language requirements in order to cast its hiring net a little wider. In this case, however, recruiters have loosened their standards for one reason and one reason only: sheer desperation. The CIA has struggled for years now with a dire shortage of officers with Arabic-language capabilities. When targeted job advertisements and linguistic recruitment goals failed to produce enough Arabic speakers, recruiters took a step back and began seeking applicants with a general aptitude for learning foreign languages and an interest in Arab culture. The CIA would, of course, prefer to hire applicants already fluent in Arabic; it is an extremely difficult language to master. However, given an increasingly severe skill shortage, recruiters had no choice but to seek *aptitude* rather than preexisting ability.

It is the best of all possible worlds when you have an ample supply of enthusiastic and well-qualified applicants for all of your job openings. As anyone who has ever had to fill an important assignment knows, however, this is rarely the case. Implementing a meaningful strategy and relaxing rigid and archaic requirements can open up a much deeper talent pool from which to draw.

A LESSON FROM THE DARK SIDE: OFFENSIVE RECRUITING

In the interest of national security, CIA officers engage in an awful lot of "recruiting" behaviors that would be illegal and downright immoral in any other context. When the circumstances warrant, they will lie, cheat, mislead, surveil, trap, threaten, and even detain. Clearly, these are not behaviors that I want readers to adopt. As a result, this chapter has focused primarily on the recruitment techniques that can be learned from the CIA's *internal* hiring practices. However, there are also lessons to be learned from the darker side— from the recruiting practices of spies and from covert operations.

Corporate hiring practices are typically reactive in nature. A position becomes vacant, advertisements go out in various media, résumés are compared, applicants are interviewed, and the best candidate gets an offer. The proliferation and success of online résumé databases has changed the paradigm somewhat, in that organizations can now search for qualified individuals at any time, and therefore no longer have to passively wait for job seekers to apply for their specific positions. So-called headhunters also tend to be less reactive; the most successful among them typically have a large stable of well-qualified individuals waiting in the wings, to be placed as appropriate jobs arise. However, in each of these cases, hiring is still done on a case-by-case basis.

What if, instead, you could cherry-pick from your competitors' best employees, thereby not only bolstering the talent set within your own organization but also dealing a harsh blow to your competitors? What if your recruiting practices focused on the most critical skill sets within your industry, and in doing so caused a crippling brain drain to impede your competition's ability to function at peak capacity?

Many readers may balk at this; "stealing" a team of employees certainly sounds unsavory. But in practice, I am not advocating anything sleazy or underhanded. Instead, you can achieve this by systematically creating a better environment for the superstars in your industry. This is akin to "stealing" customers by delivering a superior product—no better and no worse.

Begin by identifying which of your competitors has the deepest bench of talent for the function or skill set that is most critical to your organization's success. Depending on your industry and your organization's position within it, the critical function could be sales, research and development, production, or any number of skill-oriented categories. Rarely will an individual senior-level executive actually bring a true competitive advantage to an organization (although you would certainly think so from today's executive compensation packages). Instead, focus on identifying those people who *do, create,* or *change* something tangible or quantifiable. I don't intend to disparage the value of strong executive leadership, but the idea that I would like to replicate from covert operations is that of diminishing your competitor's capabilities while at the same time enhancing your own.

Next, identify the "target" who, if hired, would be most capable of helping your company build its dream team by propagating a brain drain among your competitors. You are looking for someone to create and lead a new team within your organization, so your target needs to be someone with sufficient talent, experience, and charisma to make other people *want* to work for him or her. Note that seniority alone does not mean anything; your ideal target may be someone relatively junior, but fully capable of rapid success.

Finding your "hook" with this coveted employee and the talented new hires you hope to attract is also part of the targeting process. What if your industry superstars are perfectly content with their present jobs? How will you even lure your targets to an interview, much less persuade them to accept a job? You should have a good idea of what will pique your targets' interest before you even initiate contact.

Obviously, compensation is king—at first glance. It is difficult to lure anyone without a competitive salary package. But not every organization has the luxury of doling out bigger and bigger salary packages; limited budgets and head-count capacities are a simple fact of corporate life. All the more reason, then, to study how the CIA manages to attract and retain incredibly talented individuals to perform dangerous, difficult work for far lower salaries than they are capable of making in the private sector. If you want to engage in offensive recruiting—the act of hiring talent for the purpose of adding to your organization's capabilities at the same time as you enervate your competition—you need to create an environment in which the best and the brightest *want* to work.

ORGANIZATIONAL STRATEGIES FROM THE CLANDESTINE WORLD

One of the best parts of working for the CIA is the opportunity to work with an incredibly varied, talented, and adventurous group of people. Consider the backgrounds of just a few of my former colleagues who come to mind: A former professional athlete turned investment banker who was already a millionaire when he started over near the bottom of the government pay scale. A corporate attorney fluent in Mandarin Chinese and French. An architect with a high-degree black belt and an impressive number of difficult mountain summits to her name. An Ivy League doctorate-holder who speaks five languages. A former Special Forces officer with an MBA from one of the nation's top universities. A former prosecutor whose sense of humor and gregarious personality enabled him to talk people into doing just about anything.

The CIA manages to recruit some pretty incredible individuals. The pay, though? Eh.

Of course, the CIA *is* able to offer its clandestine service employees perks that you won't find anywhere else. I, for one, was thrilled to no end by the chance to spend a week jumping out of airplanes during the agency's condensed airborne school, receive disguise training, and go through a high-speed "crash and bang" driving course that included a lesson in smashing through blockades. Never mind that these newfound skills played little to no role in my subsequent day-to-day duties—it was incredible fun! I would happily forgo a corporate bonus or two for these opportunities.

Obviously, though, the CIA is not a perfect place, and the job isn't for everyone. As with any job, there are pros and cons to the undercover profession. The bureaucracy can be maddening, advancement can be slow, and there are plenty of incompetent jerks, just like in any large organization.

Yet the clandestine service manages to retain many officers whose skills, education, and experiences would allow them to pursue their choice of opportunities in the outside world. In fact, the retention rate in the clandestine service compares very favorably to the private sector. So why do the employees stay?

A big part of the reason for the impressive retention is because of the CIA's mission. Case officers believe in what they do, and they like making a difference in the world. The travel opportunities, the glamour of the job, and the excitement also keep people around. But while these factors are not fully replicable in the corporate world, the CIA also utilizes a number of organizational strategies that can certainly be duplicated by private employers to keep talented and in-demand employees happy and productive.

The following organizational structures and strategies used by the CIA are listed not only because they appeal to high-performing *individuals*, but because they also contribute to high performance for *organizations*:

1. Encourage frequent rotation. CIA officers change assignments frequently. My own assignments have lasted everywhere from sixty-day stints in war zones with minimal infrastructure to almost three years in a more stable position. Perhaps more important, each of my assignments was drastically different from the last. For a self-confessed job-hopper such as me, this was very appealing. There was little opportunity to get bored, and ample opportunity to learn.

High performers hate stagnant environments. Small companies in particular, though, frequently face headroom limitations that make upward mobility difficult. A company with only six employees simply can't justify promoting to the management ranks everyone who shows potential; to do so would result in a top-heavy, unproductive organization. However, allowing talented employees to move between departments, functions, and locations breeds a multidimensional workforce, and also helps to circulate knowledge and talent throughout your organization. It also keeps things interesting for your employees, who might otherwise begin to feel stuck. The next item is related:

2. Be a résumé builder. Ironically, the best employers are often those who make it the easiest to find work elsewhere. That's because the top employers provide the best training opportunities, the most challenging assignments, the most capable mentors, and the most diverse experiences. The better and the more challenging the job, the better it makes as an entry on a résumé.

It's hard to beat "Clandestine Service Officer, Central Intelligence Agency" for an eyebrow-raising résumé entry. By becoming an employer recognizable in your own right for the quality and talent of your workforce, though, you become more attractive not only to the top candidates, but also to your customers and clients.

3. Match the person, not the title, to the task. After I finished my year of training to become a clandestine service officer, I reported for my first day of work expecting not much more than instructions on where to find my desk and introductions to my new colleagues. I was stunned, then, when the first words out of my new boss's mouth were, "Did you pass your firearms training?" I had—in fact I had done surprisingly well for someone who doesn't like guns— but I couldn't imagine why she was asking. It turns out that she wanted me to head to Afghanistan. As soon as possible. It was not the first day on the job that I had anticipated, but this was shortly after 9/11, so I quickly agreed to go.

Fast-forward a few blurry weeks later and I found myself—still in my twenties and barely a year out of my former corporate life— wearing a bulletproof vest and a gun, sitting in the back of a jeep driven by a heavily armed Afghan man, with my feet literally resting on a Stinger missile. This was the first of many moments when all I could do was shake my head and wonder how on earth I had come to be in that situation. I enjoyed many things about my career at the CIA, but the single best part of it was the existence of incredible opportunities and huge responsibilities from the first day I reported to duty.

If you are serious about attracting the top talent in your industry, you can't afford to let your employees languish in unchallenging positions. Too often, employers recruit bright and talented individuals, but then hesitate to give them any real responsibility until they are more "seasoned" or more senior in the organization. In the meantime, the talented recruits are bored out their minds, and likely to spend their ample free time surfing the Internet for a better job.

I'm not advocating that employers put untested new hires in situations where a beginner's mistake could be costly for the organization. I do, however, believe that employees' skills and abilities—*not* their seniority or job title—should determine who is best qualified for the most high-stakes assignments.

When the CIA identifies a high-profile target, careful attention is given to selecting the right officer for the job. Consideration is given to language, nationality, personality, gender, age, and area of expertise. It does not always make sense for a fifty-five-year-old English-speaking white male electrical engineer from Wisconsin to try to recruit a twentysomething female hijab-wearing Middle Eastern student who speaks only Arabic, for example—even if the fifty-five-year-old is a highly skilled senior officer.

Similar employee-customer "matches" are also important in the private sector, although using different criteria. I know one senior partner in a well-known law firm who still does not know how to use a computer—his secretary prints out his e-mails for him, and he dictates the responses. He is a brilliant lawyer, but he was obviously not the most appropriate legal counsel for one of the firm's most important clients—a high-tech Internet-based company. Although the law firm has a history of making hierarchy-based assignments—pairing the junior associates with the less lucrative and lower-profile clients—the managing partners finally decided that they would need to tap into some of their more tech-savvy but newer lawyers or risk losing a client that didn't want to have to explain technology basics to its high-priced legal counsel.

While it is not advisable to match customers and employees based on demographic variables like nationality, gender, or age (in fact, doing so would likely put you in violation of EEO laws) when making assignments, *do* consider an employee's personality, skill set, language capabilities, and whatever else may impress your customer. Just as CIA officers find it easier to establish rapport and trust with targets when they share something in common, so will your employees thrive when their assignments are matched to their skills. Eliminating hierarchy-based assignment practices ultimately benefits both employees *and* your relationship with your customers.

4. Spice things up. Clearly, not every work assignment is glamorous, not every client is high profile, and not every account is career enhancing. On the other hand, *every* organization has mundane work that simply needs to be done, and someone has to do it. Given this reality, it is all the more important to make sure that employee enthusiasm is not extinguished by endless dreary tasks, and that initiative is not crushed by distance from organizational power.

CIA officers lead exciting lives, but even spies need to do their accounting. Furthermore, the clandestine service is kept operational by an enormous cast of support officers. Their jobs—logistics, health, administration, and travel, among others—are not the jobs depicted in Hollywood's version of the CIA. But the functions are critical, and these folks often find themselves performing their support roles in dangerous, high-pressure environments—just like their more high-profile clandestine service colleagues.

So, how to keep support staff involved and motivated? The CIA does it by keeping support staff involved and motivated.

That is not a facetious statement. Instead, it is the best way to describe the CIA's use of cross-functional teams that include members from a wide variety of backgrounds and pay grades. (Now, hear me out and don't skip this section quite yet. I am fully aware that using cross-functional teams was in vogue in management literature a decade or two ago, and that the use of these teams was of mixed value, depending on the industry and application.) The CIA does not use cross-functional teams for the purpose of employee satisfaction, or simply as an academic exercise in trendy organizational design. Instead, it organizes groups of officers from different functions across the agency—not just the clandestine service—in order to get in, get things done, and get out as safely and efficiently as possible.

When was the last time your organization included anyone but the usual cast of executives in an important planning session? Yet the CIA would never be able to move quickly on a fast-breaking operation if it didn't involve people from across the organization. Getting one case officer in front of a high-profile target on an urgent basis requires analytical support, logistical planning, medical clearance, finance, and appropriate documents (whether forged or authentic), along with numerous other supporting elements. Your organization certainly has its own activities and events that require substantial involvement from multiple departments. So shouldn't the members of the various departments work together on a regular basis?

The CIA utilizes many different kinds of cross-functional teams. Quick-response teams drill together to be able to deploy on a moment's notice. Red Cell teams, discussed in chapter 3, combine the unlikeliest people to brainstorm the unlikeliest threats. Surveillance teams intentionally include the most diverse possible memberships so that at least one team member can blend in just about anywhere. Task forces bring in members from different government organizations, military branches, and law enforcement agencies. Career evaluation panels consisting of individuals from various ranks are used to assess officer performance. Case assessment teams bring together experts from both the analytical and the operational sides of the house. Strategic planning teams consist of members with years of field experience who have been asked to complete a headquarters-based management tour. Recruitment teams incorporate members from each of the CIA's directorates to do joint presentations for recruiting events all over the country. In each of these cases, the teams are composed of people from widely varying backgrounds who come together to accomplish a single objective.

In the highly compartmentalized atmosphere of the CIA, the formation of these teams is critical to communications, efficiency, and the achievement of results. The teams were created to function, not to educate, but members always walk away with a broader understanding of the organization (for better or for worse). And this only makes the organization stronger. Participation can be enjoyable, or it can be frustrating. Just as a group of physicists will usually walk, talk, and dress differently from a group of graphic designers, the different functions within the CIA also have distinct personalities and practices. Sometimes the clash of cultures can be distracting, and sometimes even amusing. But most important? The teams get the job done, and the members are always rewarded for their involvement. In fact, participation in multidisciplinary teams is considered crucial for promotion.

Every industry has its own specialists and its own critical skills, and cross-functional teams naturally work better in some environments than in others. Every type of organization, however, can benefit from the use of quick-response teams to deal with predictable but urgent matters. Red Cell teams to play devil's advocate and deal with unpredictable matters, and task forces to deal with the most difficult challenges with the minimum number of bureaucratic obstacles. These teams, which are designed to predict, react, and facilitate as effectively as possible in extreme circumstances, can be just as valuable in the private sector as in the CIA. Participation is rewarding for both the organization and the employees, and it keeps *everyone*—not just your superstars or senior executives—motivated and involved.

5. Make room for lone wolves. At the risk of contradicting myself after the last section extolling the virtue of teams, I hasten to advise readers not to *force* collaboration onto talented individuals who are superstars in their own right but don't necessarily work well with others. Some people thrive on team participation, out-of-specialty rotational assignments, and constant developmental opportunities. Other people do their jobs well and just want to be left alone to do what they were hired for.

I had one colleague who was a grizzled, gruff, unsmiling sort.

How he ever became a case officer was beyond me, because not only did he lack the winning personality possessed by most CIA officers, but he also seemed to quite literally dislike most other people in the world. And yet he was brilliant at his job. He possessed an encyclopedic knowledge of weapons systems and defense strategies, and he was uniquely able to spot, assess, and develop other people just like himself—targets with highly specialized knowledge who shunned most of the traditional approaches used by case officers. He excelled in getting taciturn, tough, and grizzled officials from target nations to spill their secrets, because he was just like them. I suspect that, on average, his conversations with his recruited assets consisted of a small fraction of the number of words used in parallel conversations between other officers and assets. Yet in his gruff, taciturn way he got the job done when no one else could.

This superb officer would have been a disastrous manager, though, and a thoroughly unpleasant team member. So he was promoted over the course of the years on the basis of his solo work and left alone to achieve his results.

Not all superstars are cut out for management, and not all will benefit from or contribute to teams. The best employers understand this and do not try to force these talented solo operators into roles that would detract from their individual successes. The CIA has plenty of ambitious sorts who yearn to be in senior management as soon as possible; it also has its share of clandestine officers who thrive in the independence afforded to spies in the field. (Incidentally, these field-preferring officers refer to CIA headquarters as the "Death Star," and will go to great lengths to avoid management positions there.) Fortunately, the organizational structure quite effectively accommodates both tracks.

Human resource practices within the CIA are substantially different from those within a private organization. Because of the nature of the work and the requirement for top-secret security clearances, clandestine careers can be far more intrusive and emotionally involved than a typical nine-to-five job. Moreover, CIA officers are in demand from private-sector employers, and—yes—sometimes even from foreign governments that are just as eager as we are to establish penetrations of rival intelligence services. All the more reason, then, for the CIA to employ an organizational and personnel structure that facilitates critical work while simultaneously motivating and monitoring employee performance.

Whether or not national security depends upon *your* organization's success, your workforce can benefit from some of the CIA's recruiting and organizational strategies. Whether you are hiring a CEO or a fry cook, you should have confidence that your selection process is fair, accurate, and effective. And once you have built an organization, you should put in place a structure that maximizes performance and attracts and retains top talent.

Paradoxically, however, the highest achievers can also be the most difficult to manage. For better or worse, they have the confidence to stand up to authority, the intelligence to debate, and the bravery to defy—all of which can amount to a serious management challenge. Although I said earlier in this chapter that your employees do not need to be your friends, it *is* imperative that you be able to trust their ability to make the right choices when you give them the autonomy they deserve. The next chapter, on ethics, addresses this issue in depth.

CHAPTER FIVE

Staying Clean in a Dirty World: The Ethics of Espionage

The asset chain-smoked through the turnover meeting, but did not otherwise seem fazed to learn that he would no longer be meeting with the officer who had been his handler for the past several years. Tom introduced me as the officer who would be replacing him, and then handed the asset a large envelope of cash—a substantial payment for the last several months of clandestine work.

The asset shook hands cheerfully with Tom, wished him luck in the future, and then pulled from the envelope a stack of large bills. Smiling broadly, he handed the money to Tom and said that the money was "for charity." "Perhaps you have a fund for the children of fallen CIA officers?" he asked with a wink. He was from a part of the world where bribery and kickbacks were a normal part of doing business, and it was crystal clear to me that the money was intended as a farewell gift for Tom in the form of a sizable kickback.

I didn't say a word about this exchange, during or after the meeting. I was still a junior officer, and I thought that it would be better to simply watch and see what happened to the money.

Almost immediately upon our return from the trip, then, I was pleasantly surprised to be copied on an internal e-mail from Tom earnestly describing the "generous donation" and documenting the transfer of the money to the agency's scholarship fund.

To this day, I do not know whether Tom even realized that the asset intended for him to pocket the money. I am, however, quite certain that keeping it never crossed Tom's mind for a second.

Why on earth would anyone ever trust a CIA officer? Not only are we selected in part because of our willingness and ability to tell a convincing lie, but we also receive specialized training in deception. We can expertly evade, fabricate, obscure, equivocate, distract, and just flat-out lie to your face. We understand the roles that body language, eye contact, timing, and detail play in persuasion. Add to that years of practice in our professional capacities, plus lying even to friends and family in order to maintain our cover, and it seems hard to believe that any of us even remember what the truth is.

And yet, as I stated earlier in this book, CIA officers are some of the most principled people you will ever meet.

How can this level of integrity and this skill at deception possibly coexist?

CIA clandestine service officers can simultaneously possess these two ostensibly contradictory traits because they live by a strict ethical code that keeps them clean in what can sometimes be a filthy, dirty world. In fact, the concept of integrity is pervasive throughout the agency, running like lifeblood through the veins of an organization that operates primarily in the shadows.

If undercover CIA case officers were known more for their ability to tell a lie than for their integrity, they would never be effective. Because of this, officers may manipulate or lie in order to get face-to-face with a target, but once the mask comes off, the lying stops. In order to persuade potential spies to risk their lives to reveal secrets, CIA officers have to demonstrate that they can be trusted with the information. A spy's welfare rests in his case officer's hands: sloppy tradecraft or poor security practices can get a source arrested or killed. In order to earn the trust necessary to work in the high-stakes clandestine world, then, CIA officers need to constantly demonstrate that they are trustworthy and dependable. As a result, the unwritten ethical code of the clandestine world is as strong as steel, and there are certain lines that a CIA case officer will *never* cross.

The business world, on the other hand, tends to view ethics and commerce as two distinct concepts that *can* overlap if the stars align. Companies that manage to be both profitable *and* ethical are lauded as if they had won two separate races at the same time. This chapter, however, will show how business professionals—like CIA officers—can use ethical practices to give them a distinct advantage in achieving the bottom line.

In fact, take it from someone whose career involved lying, cheating, and stealing on a daily basis: the dirtier, messier, and rougher the business, the more important it is to have strong principles and absolute standards.

HARDBALL ETHICS

Case officers don't adhere to strict ethical guidelines because to do so is "nice." In fact, case officer ethics are not rooted in humanitarian principles at all. Establishing trust is simply part of a CIA officer's job. Trust is as important to the clandestine world as capital is to the private sector—it is necessary to stay in business.

This trust is built through ongoing demonstrations of integrity and strict adherence to a code of conduct. I firmly believe that the ethical principles that guide CIA officers are 100 percent transferable to the corporate world. Unfortunately, the topic of business ethics sometimes gets a bad rap in tough markets. No one, of course, wants to act *un*ethically. However, as I was once told by a senior executive, "You won't find ethics manuals on the bookshelves of CEOs who play hardball."

The idea that adherence to strict ethical standards is somehow "soft" is further perpetuated by business ethics books that discuss the topic solely in academic, moralistic, or philosophical terms. (I still shudder when I remember grad school assignments that required analysis of tedious chapters of academic ethical theories derived from Kantian philosophy.) CIA officers, however, learn early on in their careers that earning a reputation for integrity and dependability can pay very real dividends when times are tough. Read on for a list of hardball principles and lessons that are neither soft nor theoretical:

I. Treat and protect your reputation and integrity as you would cold, hard cash. I like nice people; I really do. I am not, however, advocating that you act with integrity just because doing so is *nice*. Your reputation is an asset, because trust is a currency. You can earn it, you can grow it, you can spend it, you can gamble with it, and you can lose it. The more trust capital you have banked with a person or organization, the more you can ask of them. Remember those old bumper stickers that used to tell us to "practice random acts of kindness"? The clandestine world's version would read "practice strategic acts of trustworthiness." It may not be as warm and fuzzy, but it does serve a purpose.

2. Understand that sharks are cannibals. (Google it if you don't believe me—you'll learn more about "intrauterine cannibalism" than you ever wanted to know.) In certain industries and professions, it is considered positive to be a "shark." Lawyers who advocate aggressively for their clients are often referred to in this way, as are aggressive salespeople. There is nothing wrong with strong, bold, fearless, and decisive behavior in the workplace. Most people I know who could be considered sharks, though, tend to pursue their career goals with a single-mindedness that renders them incapable of seeing anything but the goal.

Managers often seek out sharks for their teams because, whether you like them or not, they get the job done. But these managers sometimes learn about sharks' cannibalistic tendencies the hard way—when their hard-charging employee turns on his team.

The ethical principle here is that your team members are a reflection on *you*. If you tolerate unprincipled behavior among your peers or subordinates in the interest of achieving results, you shouldn't be surprised when the sharks start circling back on you. Guess what? An employee who is willing to do anything to make a sale is also willing to do whatever it takes to get *your* job.

The CIA takes the behavior of its employees very seriously. Not only is the initial screening for all new hires rigorous, but officers are subject to frequent background and financial reinvestigations as well as regular polygraphs throughout their careers. Unprincipled conduct is referred to as a "suitability issue" in CIA parlance, because ethical lapses are understood to mean that an individual is no longer suitable for employment or security clearance. No officer wants to work with a teammate whose ethical lapses could result in disastrous consequences. "Aggressive" case officers are welcome. Sharks, on the other hand, are not.

3. Compartmentalize. The CIA is often criticized for failing to adequately share information with policy makers, the rest of the intelligence community, and the public. In some cases, this criticism is deserved. In others, information is withheld because it *must* be, for any number of reasons ranging from national security to doubts about the accuracy of the data. The general rule is that information is disseminated on a "need to know" basis.

In the corporate world, compartmentalization can serve a similar function. We all know that knowledge is power. Secrets, of course, can be incredibly powerful indeed. Just as in the clandestine world, though, you need to use your knowledge of secrets judiciously. Don't boast about your knowledge, don't spread information for malicious purposes, and don't share other people's secrets gratuitously. You lose trust capital with every loose secret, so make sure that your revelations are worth the price. (And sometimes they are *well* worth the price.)

4. Know when to lie. This is a slightly facetious way of saying just the converse—know when *not* to lie. This includes the most common type of lie within organizations—lies of omission. You should be known as someone who can take a secret to your grave (see compartmentalization, above), but also as someone who will never withhold information unnecessarily. Too many midlevel managers, in particular, treat information as a competitive advantage; they withhold it from peers and subordinates in order to have a greater share of the power. There are many reasons to withhold information, but putting your teammates at a disadvantage is not one of them.

Within the CIA, even a small lie to colleagues is considered a serious offense. Clandestine officers rely on every member of their team to keep operations running smoothly and safely. Even an inconsequential lie would cast doubts on a colleague's suitability and trustworthiness. Therefore, although officers may practice their cover stories (the elaborate lies that allow them to pursue their real agendas) with one another, they will never lie to a colleague.

You may also be surprised to hear that CIA officers try to lie as little as possible, even when dealing with targets. Generally speaking, the closer one's cover story is to the truth, the easier it is to remember, and the easier it is to defend. Because of this, a CIA officer's undercover identity will typically consist of blatant lies woven with half-truths, glued together with real facts. The closer your story is to the truth, the easier it is to convince a hostile immigration officer, a cynical target, or just a nosy stranger that you are who you say you are.

I don't mean for this to sound as if I'm encouraging readers to lie at all, whether big lies or small ones. Quite the opposite, in fact— I'm simply attempting to explain that even those people who *must* lie, like CIA officers, try to keep the mistruths to a minimum. Why risk getting caught up in a tangled web of lies when the truth will suffice?

5. Own the solution, not the mistake. Schoolyard ethics extol the virtues of admitting one's mistakes. That's all good and fine, but when the stakes are high, creating the solution is a lot more important than owning the mistake.

A CIA officer would *never* show up to a meeting with an asset to announce, "By the way, you've been compromised; we're working on it, and I'll get back to you later this week." Instead, news of a possible compromise would be accompanied by a detailed exfiltration plan, a new identity, and travel documents in hand. And yet somewhere along the line the corporate world seemed to come to a belief that simply identifying and taking credit for a mistake was laudable. Stating that you "take full responsibility" for a mistake is not a magnanimous act. Finding and implementing the fix *is*.

6. Acknowledge that personal life does reflect on business life. CIA officers aren't allowed much privacy. They have to disclose intimate relationships, submit to medical and psychological screening, and regularly take the dreaded "lifestyle" polygraph. Unlike other polygraph exams that test strictly for veracity on a very specific topic, the lifestyle polygraph requires officers to discuss excruciatingly personal topics while hooked up to the lie detection machine. It can be an unpleasant, nerve-racking experience for even the cleanest-living individuals. This mandatory confessional of sorts is such a ubiquitous part of the work culture that CIA officers often joke that "that's between you and your polygrapher" when a colleague reveals overly personal information.

Personally, I don't believe that the polygraph exams used by the CIA are particularly effective, both because there are countermeasures and because the interpretation of results is more art than science, and therefore highly subjective. That's a topic for another book, however. Yet although I am not a fan of the polygraph, I *do* believe in one of the reasons for its use—the premise that your personal life can and does reflect on your business life.

I certainly do not advocate corporate witch hunts to determine employees' foibles and faults. However, employers who become aware of issues either criminal or simply unethical should not be so quick to dismiss the impact on the organization just because the crime occurred on personal time. Spousal abusers *are* violent people, and are more likely to commit additional acts of aggression at home or at the office. Philanderers *are* more likely to conduct their liaisons on company time, or to use company funds to pay for their activities. Drug or alcohol abuse *does* impair judgment, even if an employee is sober during work hours. Racist comments posted on an employee's personal blog *do* give you fair notice that your employee is also likely to espouse the same viewpoint with co-workers.

It's simple: past behavior predicts future behavior. Disreputable behavior on personal time is an indicator of a greater likelihood of disreputable behavior on *your* clock. Character and integrity are constants, and any display of a lack thereof should be taken seriously. To combat this problem, seek out individuals who can be aggressive in a business setting but compassionate on an interpersonal level. Furthermore, don't draw an arbitrary distinction between behavior that occurs on versus off the clock. Regardless of whether you learn about unethical conduct from an employees' activities at work, a police report, or photos on a Facebook page, the take-home lesson should be the same: zero tolerance on your payroll.

7. Accept that allegiances shift. Look at Afghanistan for a classic example of shifting allegiances. Once the enemy of our Cold War enemy, this nation was treated by the United States as an ally against the USSR. Fast-forward to 2001, however, and the Stinger missiles that we provided for use against Soviet troops were now being aimed at our own soldiers, and the Russians were advising us on strategies against the Taliban.

Corporate buyouts, mergers, joint ventures, and even personnel changes can similarly result in yesterday's enemy being today's ally. Just look at the long history of JPMorgan Chase: it's a veritable soap opera of mergers and acquisitions, involving a staggering number of overlapping competitors. All the more reason, then, to demonstrate integrity even when dealing with your toughest competitors, and to maintain civility with even your most despised rivals. The world changes quickly, and it can be impossible to predict when your interests might align with some surprising players.

8. Sleep with the enemy . . . with one eye open. In a world of shifting allegiances, there are always enemies. Don't be afraid to proceed—cautiously—should a mutually beneficial opportunity to work with your enemy arise.

There are places where CIA officers simply can't go. Remember how the profile of an ideal clandestine officer is sometimes referred to as a Boy Scout with a secret dark side? Well, Boy Scouts stick out like sore thumbs in many parts of the world. Terrorists rely on this when they select their base of operations, such as when Osama bin Laden chose to make his headquarters in places like Sudan and Afghanistan—both extremely difficult environments for CIA officers to operate in. But there are a number of nations that are hostile toward both the United States *and* terrorist training camps within their borders. The CIA relies on limited partnerships with these "enemy" states to capture, detain, and sometimes extradite suspected terrorists. These joint operations often go on in spite of public animosity between the two countries.

On a (hopefully) less dramatic front, organizations should similarly be willing to partner with their "enemy"—whether that be a competitor, an unpleasant former colleague, or an investigating regulatory agency—when the benefits outweigh the risks. Protect your assets as you proceed, but be open to opportunities that may arise with the unlikeliest partners.

9. Act urgently when things are urgent. Sound like a no-brainer? Yet there are personality types and work styles that treat *everything* as a crisis. In certain organizations, a "sense of urgency" is extolled as an important virtue, even when the reality of the situation is anything *but* urgent. In many situations, rushing things can actually do more harm than good.

One of the more difficult aspects of a clandestine officer's job is knowing when a target is ready to hear a recruitment pitch. Just imagine yourself in a potential spy's shoes. Say a person with whom you have developed an increasingly close and trusting relationship suddenly tells you that she has a secret. She reveals that much of what she has told you about herself is a lie—she is actually an undercover CIA officer, and she wants *you* to risk your life and livelihood to pass her top-secret information on a regular basis. Obviously, this is not an easy request to process. An officer who rushes the developmental process and fails to establish sufficient rapport and trust runs the risk of having her target balk, refuse, or even report her to the authorities. Even when the target possesses information of an urgent nature, officers need to be careful not to unnecessarily rush the situation. To do so would be counterproductive.

Yet I have known managers in the corporate world who believe that anything *but* a sense of urgency is unacceptable. They like their employees to jump when they call, and to have all tasks completed *yesterday*. Not only does this style of management promote sloppy, rushed work, but it also abuses employees who are perfectly aware that the report that they worked on all weekend could have waited, but for their manager's impatience. It also doesn't leave room for shifting priorities. If your team members have a true grasp of what is urgent and what is not, they can instantly adapt and prioritize when something *truly* critical arises.

10. Revere the law of unintended consequences. CIA officers are always on the lookout for political, economic, and even industrial changes that may have indirect consequences for targets of interest. A military coup somewhere, for example, means that there are suddenly quite a few former senior officials who have been displaced from power, and are likely both to carry a grudge against the new regime and be in need of a new paycheck. In other words, they are ripe for recruitment. Nepotism also yields benefits for case officers on the prowl for new spies. When a country's leader appoints his son-in-law to a prominent position rather than the career official who has been toiling for years in hope of a promotion, there is suddenly a disgruntled official just waiting for a visit from his friendly U.S. government representative.

The corporate world can also take advantage of unintended consequences. Your competitor is considering possible layoffs? Now is the time to siphon off their top talent—even those who will likely be immune from layoffs will be eager to find more stable employment. Lawsuits and unfavorable regulatory rulings against your suppliers may mean that they are more eager than ever to lock in long-term contracts at discounted rates. A senior partner at the competing law or consulting firm gets bad publicity in the local press? Once-loyal clients are suddenly willing to consider switching.

Make it a point to keep current on local and industrial news, with the intention of extrapolating unintended consequences with potential benefit for you or for your organization. This is also yet another example of where you can benefit from having an extended network of contacts within your industry: the earlier you learn of impending changes, the faster you can act. Senior personnel moves, legal rulings, changing market conditions, and many other changing variables throughout your competition's supply chain and customer pool can all have positive consequences for you.

Is this predatory? A bit, perhaps. Would your competition happily return the favor if the circumstances were reversed? Of course.

11. Take responsibility for the integrity of your supply chain. The CIA gets a lot of information from an extremely wide variety of sources. Some of that information is accurate, urgent, and of major consequence. Some is decidedly not. All clandestine officers have to learn to sort out the accurate information from the erroneous. Information can be bad for myriad reasons: sometimes sources struggle with language barriers, sometimes they fabricate or lie in the hope of receiving payment for false information, and—surprisingly often—information comes from delusional individuals who harbor conspiracy theories involving the CIA. (The agency's public Web site, in particular, receives some unbelievably off-the-wall e-mails.) One of my colleagues had to maintain a straight face during a meeting with a potential "source" who reported that Osama bin Laden was living in Florida and had managed to escape detection because he went everywhere dressed as a clown, with full face makeup including a red rubber nose. The source claimed to know this because of his psychic abilities.

Fortunately, the overwhelming majority of incoming information is not quite so bizarre. Nevertheless, not all sources are created equal, and determining whether a report is legitimate can be difficult. When reporting collected information to the intelligence community, then, CIA officers have a responsibility to notify recipients about factors that cast doubt on the credibility of a source's report. Clearly, a report from a semicoherent drunk with an obvious goal of seeking political asylum should not be given as much weight as a report from someone whose demeanor and supporting details indicate a high likelihood that the source is telling the truth.

The corporate world also bears a responsibility to its consumers to continually evaluate its sources. Companies like Nike and Reebok learned the hard way that consumers *will* blame them for having subcontractors who use child labor; plausible deniability did not appease company critics for a second. Mattel, among other major toy companies, has had to recall millions of toys because Chinese suppliers used lead paint. Clearly, this was *not* a high point for the company's brand reputation. The topic of evaluating suppliers will be covered in more detail later in the book, but suffice it to say that it behooves both the CIA *and* the private sector to constantly and carefully evaluate sources.

12. Count your nickels and dimes. The clandestine world is a cash economy. After all, a spy can't exactly accept a personal check, right? Because of this, CIA officers have access to large sums of cash, and a great deal of discretion in how it is spent. They also have quite a few expenses that would be, well, *unusual* in the corporate world. For example, I had a colleague who received approval to use government funds for eyebrow waxing, because the CIA disguise team decided that her dark, distinctive eyebrows made it too difficult to alter her appearance when necessary.

Perhaps *because* it would be so easy for an officer to filch a little money here and a little money there, even the tiniest of financial irregularities are grounds for immediate dismissal. Case officers are very aware that they are spending taxpayer dollars, and they don't mess around with their cash or their accounting. Moreover, this goes back to the principle that even small ethical lapses are indicative of character flaws and integrity issues that can render an individual unsuitable for employment in a job that requires as much trust as the CIA.

The corporate world, on the other hand, regularly suffers from very well-publicized integrity lapses in the form of inappropriate spending. Former Tyco International CEO Dennis Kozlowski, for example, who was convicted in 2005 for misappropriation of corporate funds. His spending habits, which included using Tyco funds to pay for a million-dollar-plus birthday party for his wife, and for his now-infamous $6,000 shower curtains, received incredulous media attention. In 2008, the CEOs of the big three U.S. automakers, GM, Chrysler, and Ford, were publicly shamed for using luxury private jets to fly to Washington, D.C., in order to plead for public funds to avoid bankruptcy. (And no, of course they did not carpool—each CEO traveled in his own jet.) That same year the public was furious to learn that millions of dollars of government-funded bailout money for the financial sector was used to pay hefty bonuses to some of the very same Wall Street investment bankers whose trading and investment activities had led to the collapse that prompted the bailout. Taxpayers scratched their heads with a feeling of outraged déjà vu when in 2011 reports came out detailing the multimillion-dollar bonuses paid to top executives of Fannie Mae and Freddie Mac for decidedly less than stellar performance during a period when both organizations were still very much dependent upon ongoing federal bailouts.

In each case, the expenditures quite understandably elicited ridicule and anger from taxpayers and shareholders toward the respective companies. It was clear to people on the outside that these events demonstrated more than just frivolous spending—they suggested serious and systemic ethical problems that eroded public trust in the organizations in question.

Clearly, a company does not go from scrupulous fiscal responsibility to writing off millions of dollars of luxury overnight. Instead, inappropriate expenditures of this magnitude come from a pervasive lack of respect for the source and purpose of funds. Nickels and dimes misspent can all too quickly become millions of dollars misspent, so principled accounting and financial practices should be adopted at all levels of an organization in order to avoid this slippery slope.

DEALING WITH ETHICAL CHALLENGES

It's easy to preach ethics in a book. It can be far more challenging to practice principled behavior in a competitive field where it seems like everyone else is playing dirty. The best strategy is to have firm, resolute principles and an unwavering boundary that you never cross.

The real world is never black and white, though, and even the strongest ethical beliefs can start to blur when the situation gets messy and gray. Prior to 9/11, for example, most CIA officers had never even heard of waterboarding. One day and four airplanes later, however, traditional agency tactics were turned on their head overnight. This is not the book to discuss or debate CIA interrogation techniques, but suffice it to say that for many of those directly involved in managing the aftermath of 9/11, what had once seemed unfathomable suddenly became a grim reality. Suddenly officials had to make decisions about how far to go during interrogations of terrorist detainees, or whether or not to render a captured terrorist to a country known to commit human rights violations. I can assure you that *no one* took these subjects lightly, and that there has never been a firm internal consensus on tough subjects such as these.

The corporate world may not have to debate the definition of torture, but many decisions made in the private sector *do* have life-

and-death implications. Pharmaceutical trials, environmental impact studies, medical insurance policy decisions, safety standards . . . there are plenty of difficult topics in the business world that have profound consequences for people's lives and livelihoods.

To make matters more complicated, the law does not always give clear instructions to guide corporate behavior. The law has loopholes, ambiguities, conflicting precedents, and unexplored territories. For some multinational transactions, it isn't even always clear which country's laws apply. Furthermore, depending on your organization's risk tolerance, the urgency of the situation, the importance of the matter, the impact on others, and the norms of the industry, you might have a very different threshold than another reader in a different business climate.

Given these complexities, it isn't always easy to identify, much less pursue, the "right" path. As CIA officers know all too well, in the midst of a dirty world, it can be difficult to stay clean. All the more reason, then, to identify and honor your ethical absolutes. You never know when your business may depend upon it.

CHAPTER SIX

Crisis Management Strategies (from an Organization That Truly Knows the Meaning of Crisis)

On September 11, 2001, I was sitting in a conference room along with the rest of my fellow clandestine service trainees. We were listening to a panel of guest speakers; the visiting presenters were various Pentagon officials talking to us about CIA cooperation with the military. Suddenly the course director walked in and announced that an airplane had just flown into one of the Twin Towers in New York City. He commandeered the remote control for the room's audiovisual system, turned on the television, and grimly left the room.

We all, of course, assumed that the announcement was part of yet another mock training exercise—just like the dozens that we had already completed. The speakers chuckled, thinking that they had been included in a surprise instructional scenario. The trainees didn't even blink; we were mere weeks away from the end of our year of training, and we were weary. We waited patiently for the drill to be further explained.

Then the beeping started. Cell phones aren't allowed in CIA buildings, but pagers are. In rapid succession, our guest speakers checked their pagers and then rushed from the room, all looking stunned.

It took several more minutes of horrible live footage playing out on the screen at the front of the room for the rest of us to realize that this time it wasn't a drill. This time, the crisis was real.

Several years before 2001 I was a trainee in a very different program. I was in a management development program within a large high-tech company—a position that I started straight out of grad school. The job was supposed to be prestigious—it was billed as a "fast track" to more senior management positions. Unfortunately, my timing was lousy. Unbeknownst to me, the dot-com bubble that had made the high-tech world so alluring to my fellow recent graduates and me had sprung a leak. Although numerically speaking the bubble wouldn't actually burst for a while, certain parts of the technology sector were already feeling the pain. Within weeks of my first day of work, my employer began to stumble. Layoffs were rumored, and then announced. An entire division was spun off, and then another division was just plain sold off.

My first rotation in the management development program was in the executive compensation department. One of my first tasks during this rotation was to decipher the complex golden parachute that was waiting for the chief executive officer. There wasn't much actual work being done elsewhere in the company as people waited to see whether or not they still had jobs, but I kept busy poring over a thick legal contract and turning it into a one-page "if-then" PowerPoint version of what would happen, financially speaking, should the CEO quit, retire, or be fired under various conditions.

The circumstances that caused my employer's plummet were not, of course, as devastating as a terrorist attack, but the company was definitely in crisis.

My respective experiences as a junior employee within two organizations in crisis could not have been more different. The crisis triggers might have been drastically dissimilar, and the stakes might have been worlds apart, but organizational psychology is filled with constants, and there are many universal reactions when a person's livelihood is threatened.

In my subsequent work as a federal investigator for the National Labor Relations Board (I told you that I job-hopped a lot!), I observed many more companies in crisis. I investigated all shapes and sizes of labor strikes, accusations of union vote fraud, allegations of picket line violence, threats from supervisors, unlawful terminations, and illegal management surveillance of union meetings. I saw organizations that responded productively and purposefully to perceived threats, and I also witnessed counterproductive, foolish, and sometimes outright criminal reactions. During the course of my investigations, I observed some of the ugliest and also some of the most collaborative reactions to organizational threats.

I am spelling out my firsthand experience with organizational crises because, based on my personal observations of numerous entities in the midst of major changes and predicaments, the CIA responded significantly more effectively, more quickly, more flexibly, and more positively than any of the other organizations I observed. Yes, the CIA made mistakes in the aftermath of 9/11—some of them tragic. But on an organizational level, its crisis management cannot be beat, and I am convinced that the private sector could learn a valuable lesson from the clandestine world's response to a crisis.

Listed here are some of the ways that the CIA responded more effectively to a crisis than what I have witnessed in the corporate world.

In its immediate reaction to 9/11, the CIA:

- Focused attention and action outward instead of inward
- Continued to acknowledge and reward performance
- Made senior management more accessible than ever
- Articulated crystal-clear directives
- Handed out extraordinary empowerment
- Redirected and refocused resources
- Went to great lengths to protect employees on the ground
- Created loyalty by inspiring it and trust by earning it

These crisis management strategies may be listed here as separate items, but they are all very much interrelated. In fact, as I wrote this book I originally attempted to create a fancy flow chart or graphic display of the CIA's response to the 9/11 crisis in order to depict how each factor strengthened the others. My relationship chart, however, very quickly became a convoluted spiderweb that would most certainly make readers' eyes glaze over. I won't torture your eyesight with the insult of an overly complicated graphic, but I *will* endeavor to articulate how every response to a crisis can and will impact subsequent actions.

CRISIS MANAGEMENT STRATEGY I: FOCUS ATTENTION OUTWARD

Finger-pointing began within hours after the events of 9/11. The entire world wanted to know who could have possibly committed such atrocities. One of the logical follow-on questions, then, was who could have *prevented* the attacks. As details began to emerge and the perpetrators were identified, the CIA fell into the crosshairs of an angry, wounded public. As we all know now in retrospect, more could have been done to prevent the events of 9/11. Information should have been shared more effectively, emerging terrorist groups should have been neutralized when we had the chance, and dots should have been connected.

At the time, however, those of us in the CIA didn't have time for blame or recriminations. Every last employee was too busy responding. From the special operations officers who deployed to Afghanistan even before the military, to the support employees who worked around the clock at headquarters for months on end without a break, everyone was focused on finding, capturing, and bringing to justice the individuals who had planned and conducted the attacks. All attention was focused outward, toward achieving the final objective.

This experience was worlds apart from what I have observed in the private sector. In the corporate world, the focus during times of crisis tends to be overwhelmingly internal. Once it becomes clear to everyone that their company is going downhill fast, productivity grinds to a screeching halt. After all, no one knows if they are going to have a job the next day, much less whether or not their projects will continue. Everyone continues to show up to work, but chances are high that if you see someone busily working at a computer, he or she is drafting a résumé or searching the Web for a new job. In my experience, this was not just true at the junior employee level; the executives were also focused on their own careers rather than the salvation of the company. (The executive compensation department at my first employer was kept humming with a dramatic uptick in requests for information about the disposition of deeply underwater stock options.) Unfortunately, an internal focus during a crisis can be a destructive morale crusher.

I am aware that, to a large extent, I am comparing apples and oranges. Whereas a crisis brought on by a terrorist attack represents a threat to one's life and one's nation, a company crisis due to changing market conditions typically impacts little more than one's employment status. But when a company in turmoil fails to rally its employees to maintain an outward focus, its negative trajectory becomes steeper and steeper.

In order to accomplish an outward focus during times of crisis, it is absolutely necessary for organizations to uphold the following three standards:

1. Brutal honesty. In most cases, the rumors that circulate during an organizational crisis are at least as bad, if not worse, than the reality. If you keep your employees apprised of the good, the bad, and the ugly, you allow them to spend more time on their work and less time speculating about what *might* be happening around them.

2. A sense of purpose. Employees with an uncertain future in an organization with an uncertain future need a unifying, motivating sense of purpose. If an organization is already being brutally honest, then management can also set brutally realistic goals: to stay in business for one more week, to slow the losses, to prevent additional negative publicity, and so on. These goals may sound depressing, but at least they give employees something to strive toward in the midst of chaos, and a sense of pride for continuing achievement.

3. Realistic commitments. It is exceedingly difficult for employees to keep an outward focus if they are worried about their ability to provide food and shelter for their families. Retention bonuses are helpful during an organizational crisis, but they are not, of course, always realistic for small employers or organizations whose financial state does not allow for the expense. Organizations in crisis therefore need to make realistic minimum commitments that will allow nervous employees to focus on the job, instead of the job search. Whether that involves a commitment to avoid layoffs for a week at a time, a commitment to pay generous bonuses once (if) the crisis abates, or a commitment to severance packages, employers need to make whatever commitments possible to ensure that employees' personal needs don't surmount organizational needs.

Keeping an outward focus during an organizational crisis ensures continuing productivity, maintenance of customer service standards, and a more positive corporate image to people inside and outside of your organization. It can also foster purpose, urgency . . . and hope. In addition, an outward focus enhances other crisis management responses:

- An outward focus **protects your frontline employees** from infighting, stress from uncertainty, and misplaced blame.
- An outward focus allows for successes to be measured and for **performance to be rewarded** even during a crisis.
- An outward focus serves as a platform for **clear directives** and **communication** as everyone rallies toward a common goal.

CRISIS MANAGEMENT STRATEGY 2: CONTINUE TO ACKNOWLEDGE AND REWARD PERFORMANCE

Organizations in crisis tend to take on a sort of collective depression. A sense of malaise and indifference sets in, and performance begins a downward spiral. Compounding this tendency, rewards and accolades for a job well done often fall to the bottom of the priority list as organizations struggle to stay afloat.

In the aftermath of 9/11, it would have been understandable for CIA performance rewards to have gone by the wayside; to some degree the act of thwarting another attack should have been motivation and reward enough on its own, right? Yet CIA management continued to acknowledge and extol successes. Details of accomplishments in the field were shared on a regular basis, and high honors were handed out regularly to much-deserving heroes. Not only did this boost the morale of the CIA officers who were facing danger and personal hardships on the front line in Afghanistan, but it also instilled a sense of organizational pride and inclusiveness among the many headquarters-based employees who were far removed from the front line but were putting in long, stressful hours themselves.

I was in Kabul, Afghanistan, in early 2002. The pace of work was grueling, the living conditions stark, and the risks were constant. Amid the chaos of a war zone, though, came small perks that made a world of difference to people working on the front line. Small luxuries were sent at great expense by the CIA to employees in the field: Starbucks coffee beans. Pringles. Ingredients for a holiday dinner on Easter. Magazines. It doesn't sound like much, but these little gifts were always accompanied by notes of appreciation, and the value of the gesture was far greater than the sum of the parts.

In most companies in crisis, on the other hand, the little perks are the first to go. Free sodas in the office refrigerator are eliminated during budget cuts. Once-lavish office holiday parties turn into potluck celebrations, or, worse yet, employees are required to buy tickets to defray the costs of the annual gala. (Note to managers: Please. Don't. Ever. Do. This. If your organization can't afford a party, then neither can your employees. They are saving their money in case you decide to lay them off.) I once worked with a company that required employees to bring their own pens from home; the office manager claimed that employee carelessness with office-issued pens was costing the organization too much money.

During organizational crises, stinginess does not only appear in the form of these morale-deteriorating but minimally effective cost cuts. Compliments and accolades also tend to vanish when a management team is under stress. Senior management may bear the brunt of organizational crises, but ceasing to motivate and acknowledge your subordinates means that you have stopped performing one of your most important roles at a time when your company can least afford it.

Take it from someone who nearly wept with gratitude when those gourmet coffee beans showed up after far too long drinking only weak tea or wretched instant coffee: rewards and incentives are more effective than ever during a crisis.

By continuing to acknowledge and reward performance, you can enhance your other crisis management techniques in several ways:

- Acknowledgment of accomplishments provides an opportunity to accompany bad news with good news during critical communication from senior management.
- Continued rewards, even small ones, provides an opportunity to **create loyalty by inspiring it**. During one of my interactions with a company in crisis, I worked with a group of employees who positively revered their boss. Why? Because he made a point to order in pizza, at personal expense, every time the group had to work late. Their company was in the middle of a devastating product recall, so late nights were common. This small gesture made a big difference to the employees on the front line of the recall.
- Rewards and acknowledgments make it easier to **redirect and refocus resources.** You are less likely to hear your employees protest that "that's not *my* job" if you are rewarding them for working outside of their normal job descriptions during times of crisis.

CRISIS MANAGEMENT STRATEGY 3: MAKE SENIOR MANAGEMENT MORE ACCESSIBLE THAN EVER

After 9/11, senior CIA officials had a lot of explaining to do, even before they had much information to explain. They had to explain to the media. They had to explain to Congress. They had to explain to closed committees, military officials, law enforcement, and foreign governments. They had to explain to the president.

With this kind of pressure, it might have been understandable if they had left employees to manage on their own for a while.

But they didn't.

In fact, George Tenet, the CIA director at the time, became famous for tromping through the cubicles of the CIA counterterrorism center with the now-infamous unlit cigar in his mouth, asking even junior officers to report extemporaneously on the latest developments. Other senior officials issued regular, formal updates that went to a wider audience than ever before—they recognized that this was not the time to compartmentalize. *All* of the CIA's employees were now involved in the hunt for terrorists. Senior management was more visible than ever before, communicating both successes and setbacks.

This visibility and accessibility of senior management contrasts sharply with my first experience with organizational crisis in the private sector. During that experience, I worked in a cubicle just around the corner from Executive Row. Just before layoffs started (although well after *rumors* of impending layoffs had started), my neighboring colleagues and I used to play a game called "spot the CEO." This would sound laughable if it wasn't true: members of the company's senior management team seemed literally to go into hiding. They arrived late and left late. They avoided eye contact and walked briskly. They entered silently and grimly, and they kept their office doors closed. I can commiserate, somewhat—it must be terrible to know before anyone else that the fate of thousands of employees' careers is in the lurch.

I witnessed this same phenomenon in other organizations over the years. During times of stress and uncertainty, senior executives often go to ground. Sometimes it is because there are legal implications and they can't divulge information prematurely. Other times it's because the future of the company is uncertain and they don't want to communicate anything until they know for sure. In one case, it was because one of the executives was facing serious criminal charges. Unfortunately, avoiding difficult questions does nothing to assuage a crisis—rather, it just fuels the rumor mills.

If senior CIA officials could manage to maintain visibility and to communicate frequently and honestly during the post-9/11 maelstrom, then surely so could management in the corporate world. If nothing else, it is a point of honor during a crisis: bad news should be communicated directly, honestly, and in a timely manner, by whoever is in command. A crisis—*any* type of crisis—is not the time for leaders to hunker down.

Maintaining senior management accessibility facilitates several of the other crisis management strategies:

- When information comes from the top, employees have the opportunity to hear **clear directives** straight from the source, rather than filtered through layers of intermediate management.
- Accessibility **instills trust** when the workforce sees that senior officials are personally invested in getting through times of organizational crisis.
- Within organizations suffering from the shackles of bureaucracy (i.e., most organizations with more than one employee), unmistakable directives that come straight from

the top official help clear the way to **redirect and refocus resources.**

CRISIS MANAGEMENT STRATEGY 4: ARTICULATE CRYSTAL-CLEAR DIRECTIVES

In late 2001 and early 2002, CIA officers heading to Afghanistan in the aftermath of 9/11 were given a very clear directive: to capture or kill Al Qaeda terrorists. For the seasoned special operations officers who hit the ground first, this was a logical order. We were at war, after all, against the people who had committed a horrible act of terrorism on U.S. soil. Still, when I arrived in Kabul mere weeks after finishing my training, this directive—given to me within an hour of arriving in Afghanistan—was startling, to put it mildly. I didn't have any military experience, and the gun that I had just been issued felt unfamiliar and uncomfortable. I am far more corporate than I am commando, and my very presence in a war zone felt surreal.

Yet there it was. A directive that couldn't be any clearer. *My* job was not to literally do any of the capturing or killing; I was only responsible for collecting the intelligence that would support this effort. Still, up until now, my "first day on the job" experiences had been limited largely to learning my way around the building and trying to locate office supplies. To be given such a brutally blunt objective from the grizzly, bearded deputy chief of station shocked me deeply. It's not that I was naïve (well, perhaps a bit)—I knew what I was getting into when I agreed to deploy to Kabul. It's just that this directive was *so* blunt that it really brought home the gravity of the situation. It was a sobering moment.

The corporate world has seen plenty of its own crises recently. But in many of the industries hardest hit (that would be *you*, automotive, financial services, and real estate sectors), senior leadership came out of the gate seemingly in denial about the gravity of the situation. Instead of acknowledging the crisis and issuing blunt directives in hopes of reversing course, the organizations delivered mixed messages to employees, shareholders, and Congress. They predicted near-term improvements while asking for bailouts; they spent lavishly on some things (corporate jets and year-end bonuses) while simultaneously cutting costs and downsizing; they promised innovation while putting projects on hold. I have an acquaintance (who shall remain nameless, because he has thus far managed to hold on to his management position in a well-known, and fast-sinking, financial services company) who describes his department as being "like the Wild Wild West":

> No one knows what to do, because we aren't getting any specific information from above. So half the office sits around and does nothing, and the other half is running around trying out all sorts of half-baked ideas in the hopes that they'll be seen as stars once the crisis blows over. It's chaos.

A chaotic organization is not, of course, well equipped to respond to a crisis.

As I stated earlier in this chapter, midcrisis is not the time for senior management to go AWOL. Not only should company officials be more accessible than ever, but they also need to be blunter and clearer than ever when issuing directives. After all, organizations in crisis are filled with employees who have a vested interest in trying to help turn things around.

Let them help.

To do this, you don't need to become a military commander overnight. You don't need to write flowery speeches, fake your way through insincere corporate pep rallies, or start spouting motivational platitudes. Instead, effective crisis leadership simply requires honest, clear, prompt, realistic, and, yes, blunt communication. It's actually quite straightforward, and should involve as many members of your organization as possible:

1. Honestly communicate the gravity of the situation.
2. Honestly communicate the options—even when there are few.
3. Narrowly define the short-term crisis management strategy, down to the departmental or even individual level, if possible.
4. Define more broadly the midrange goals.
5. Update often.

The third item is the most important in a crisis, as this is the step that enables your employees to act, to help, to produce. Make your instructions clear, empowering, and unmistakable, and then step back to let the members of your organization do their jobs.

I sincerely doubt that senior CIA officials thought of their communications as formally as this section may imply. Instead, their successful communication strategy emerged organically from a sincere desire and a frank need for every member of the organization to immediately hear, know, and act on breaking information as it developed.

Crystal-clear directives enhance other crisis management strategies as well:

- The clearer the objectives are, the more you can **empower** your employees to act above and beyond their normal capacities.
- Identifying and articulating clear directives during a crisis **inspires loyalty** by demonstrating effective management during a crisis.

- Clear, actionable directives help keep **an outward focus** and maintain productivity.

CRISIS MANAGEMENT STRATEGY 5:
HAND OUT EXTRAORDINARY EMPOWERMENT

Unlike for most private organizations in crisis, money was not an issue for the CIA after 9/11. War is a cash economy, and fortunately for us, cash was abundant. In Afghanistan we paid cash for tactical intelligence. We paid cash for informants. We paid cash for protection, and cash for real estate. We paid cash to buy back the Stinger missiles that we had given out back when we thought that the Soviets were the bigger threat. Officers were given funds in chests, boxes, and bags. We were responsible for providing receipts and accounting for the money that we handed out, of course, but it was still sometimes a bit dizzying to see so many bills all at once. I remember once hesitating to sign a receipt for a large brown bag full of cash that I was to deliver to a local Afghan warlord for his cooperation; I was signing my responsibility for a value that exceeded my yearly salary. I wanted to read the fine print first, but in a war zone there are no lawyers and there is no fine print.

Even among the more experienced CIA officers deployed to Afghanistan, the level of empowerment was unprecedented. Most of the officers on the ground were given far more funding and far more responsibility than they had ever had in their careers. They were given the authority and the means to accomplish a herculean task, and they did it well.

The empowerment given to officers on the front line also changed a long-standing, somewhat destructive organizational dynamic. The CIA's clandestine service has long been marked by a barely disguised antipathy between headquarters and the field. Headquarters, or the "Death Star," is reviled by field-based officers for its risk aversion, glacial pace, and mind-numbing meetings. Headquarters "weenies" are criticized for being naïve, unsupportive, and bureaucratic. Case officers in the field, on the other hand, are criticized for being overly aggressive, impetuous, and prone to action without understanding the big picture.

Keep in mind that CIA clandestine officers rotate jobs frequently, so most headquarters officers have spent plenty of time in the field, and vice versa. It doesn't matter. The moment officers begin their latest job—whether at headquarters or overseas—they become one of "them."

This us-versus-them mentality all but vanished during the period after 9/11. Field-based officers were permitted to make significant commitments and decisions without having to cable back to headquarters for permission. Headquarters invited the field to make wish lists of supplies, funding, authorizations, people, and gear—and then provided everything that the field requested. Immediately. It was this extraordinary empowerment that enabled those officers who deployed to Afghanistan first to make extraordinary progress in a very difficult situation.

Now, let's compare this to what tends to happen to a corporation in crisis. Because abundant funding is typically *not* an option for troubled organizations, expenditures are often the first decisions to be bumped up to a more senior level. Suddenly, junior managers are required to get authorization before booking a plane ticket. Customer service representatives have to seek management approval before granting customer refunds. Conference attendance fees are reconsidered at a higher level. Performance bonuses have to be signed off on personally by the CEO.

When a crisis is financial in nature, this is understandable, of course. But disempowerment can be a slippery slope. A company on thin ice, financially speaking, tends to become increasingly conservative in *all* matters. Marketing plans are deemed too risky, given the circumstances. Building expansion is curtailed. A hiring freeze goes into effect. These decisions to cut back, hold off, delay, and reduce come from higher and higher. The employees on the front line lose nearly all ability to commit or act. Ultimately, extraordinary *dis*empowerment leads to an extraordinary inability to perform.

Empowerment in a time of crisis is risky. When the future of your organization is on the line, every decision and every commitment takes on a monumental importance. But if you can't trust those employees on the front line—meaning those employees who deal most closely with your customers—to continue to make the right decisions in a time of crisis, then your hiring, training, and management practices are so flawed that your organization may very well be doomed to fail, regardless of senior-level intervention. The CEO can't flip every burger.

I hope that by now I have established that I have a seething hatred for buzzwords. In grad school I used to play "buzzword bingo" with my classmates—we created bingo cards with the business jargon du jour, and we'd cross out the words as the lecturer uttered them. Any card with the word "strategic" was a ringer for sure, since business professors use that word more often than a teenager says "like." "Empowerment" was another ubiquitous term, and therefore one that I hesitated to use here. To clarify, then, I need to emphasize that I do not use the word "empowerment" in a namby-pamby, feel-good-about-yourself kind of way. I am referring to something specific and concrete. Extraordinary empowerment means granting more decision-making authority, and more *control*, than ever to employees on lower rungs of the corporate ladder. A time of crisis is the time to let the experts—those who have been doing the job day-to-day since well before the crisis—do what they do best.

Extraordinary empowerment enhances several other crisis management strategies:

132

- It allows your employees to *do something* to help allay the crisis, and thereby maintain an **external focus**.
- Empowering all ranks of your organizations allows senior leadership to be **more accessible than ever**, because they are free to lead rather than micromanage.
- Extraordinary empowerment allows you to **redirect and refocus** resources, because it allows your employees the authority to do more than ever before.

CRISIS MANAGEMENT STRATEGY 6: REDIRECT AND REFOCUS

Immediately after 9/11, CIA officers started to come out of the woodwork. There literally were not enough desks or computer monitors to accommodate all of the officers who came in to do work well outside of their job descriptions. They donated their time after completing their day-to-day duties, giving up their evenings and weekends. Retired officers and officers who had resigned from the agency years before came back to offer their services. Officers gave up plum overseas assignments to return to relatively less glamorous but now-critical headquarters positions in the agency's Counterterrorism Center. Trainees wrapped up long, strenuous days of surveillance detection classes and then headed into headquarters at night to help out in any way possible. In the chaotic aftermath of the terrorist attacks, job descriptions meant very little. If you were there, you were capable, and you were willing, then you were put to work.

Once the dust started to settle somewhat, it became clear that life

WORK LIKE A SPY

at the CIA would never be the same again. The agency's mission, methodology, and mind-set were drastically and irrevocably altered. For decades the stars of the clandestine world had been the Cold War warriors—those officers who spoke Russian, had spent their careers chasing and being chased by the KGB, and had developed a taste and a tolerance for vodka. But after 9/11, the skill sets that served officers well for Iron Curtain operations suddenly seemed quaint, overly cerebral, and excessively regimented.

The new superstars? The new hotshots in the clandestine world were the officers who spoke Arabic, Farsi, and Dari. They were more familiar with the social intricacies associated with sharing a cup of tea than a bottle of vodka. And whereas it used to be the rare clandestine officer who ever handled a firearm, suddenly weapons training became mandatory. (Imagine my bemusement when I discovered that my own, hastily organized M4 assault rifle qualification course was also attended by a sweet, diminutive grandmother of three!) Officers traded custom-tailored suits for Kevlar, and it became common to overhear casual hallway conversations about the pros and cons of the different types of antimalarial medications.

The CIA's clandestine service had to reinvent itself after 9/11, and this was no small undertaking. The change in the agency's focus required changes to nearly every aspect of business—training, hiring, logistics, technology. Without a hint of nostalgia, the clandestine service stepped up and began a metamorphosis that isn't yet complete more than a decade later.

The corporate world is certainly no stranger to reinvention either. Some drastic changes in focus are strategic—an effort to capture a new market segment, for example—while at other times they come from necessity and/or crisis. As the innumerable consulting firms that claim to be experts in change management can attest, reinvention is risky. (Anyone remember Starbucks' brief foray into home decor and furniture? I thought not.) But whatever the impetus for change, the simple fact is that once you go, there's no going back.

The CIA's reinvention was not seamless, of course, but the agency did manage to redirect and refocus its resources quickly, effectively, and intelligently. Here are some of the strategies used by the CIA that could apply equally well in any organization:

I. Make assignments based on skill set, not job title. After 9/11, the CIA urgently needed specific language skills, paramilitary capabilities, and target-specific technology. Because the critical skill sets were not abundant within the agency, officers with these capabilities were put immediately into positions of leadership. In a crisis, let skills and abilities supersede seniority. When your company's computers crash, the executives stand back and let the IT experts do their jobs, don't they? The same deference should apply to anyone who has the skills to get your organization out of a jam—whether the critical skill set resides in the HR department, such as during a strike, in accounting during an audit, or in the marketing department when bad publicity hits. The most successful leaders know when to lead, and when to stand back and let their experts run the show.

2. Deploy agile teams to work autonomously in the field, unencumbered by the bureaucratic quicksand back home. This is where the quick-response teams mentioned in chapter 4 come in handy. Get employees with critical skill sets away from the organizational obstacles and slowdowns that always accompany large changes. Give them the resources and the authority to do their jobs, and then fill them in on the changes back home later.

3. Let go of the past without sentimentality. In the wake of 9/11, the CIA needed its officers—*all* of its officers—to focus on the terrorist threat. The agency may have had plenty of funding, but it did not possess an abundance of officers with the appropriate skill sets.

Senior officials operated with brutal efficiency to declare that certain regions of the world, certain targets, certain languages, and certain programs were no longer needed. Funding was diverted, assignments were curtailed, and programs were canceled. The impacted people and resources were still needed; they were just needed *elsewhere*. These changes affected junior and senior officers alike, and those who didn't like the new reality were invited to look for a new career. Corporate changes—particularly those induced by crisis—can and should be just as thorough, definitive, and comprehensive as the CIA's.

Redirecting and refocusing corporate resources in order to respond effectively to a crisis overlaps significantly with a couple of the CIA's other crisis management strategies:

- By redirecting and refocusing resources, you are—by definition—articulating a **crystal-clear directive** to change.
- By refocusing and redirecting, you are **empowering** your workforce by giving them the resources they need to operate in the new reality.

CRISIS MANAGEMENT STRATEGY 7: PROTECT THE EMPLOYEES ON THE GROUND

To say that CIA officers in post-9/11 Afghanistan were busy would be like saying that Enron executives had a small habit of fibbing—both are dramatic understatements. CIA officers back at Langley's headquarters were also busy—*very* busy. Not only were they providing twenty-four-hour support to critical and sensitive field operations, but they were also feverishly responding to congressional and Executive Office requests for briefings, after-action reports, and analysis. The requests were perfectly valid (mostly), but they were also often redundant, time-consuming, and never-ending. The requests came in with priorities ranging from immediate to yesterday. *Everything* was urgent.

For the most part, CIA headquarters did an admirable job of protecting its frontline employees—those officers deployed to Afghanistan—from the furor back home. The finger-pointing, retroactive quests for accountability, and endless requests for data stayed back home so that the employees on the ground could accomplish their primary mission and stay safe doing so. The only symptoms of bureaucracy that slipped through were the fairly regular CODELS— congressional delegations that often involved a sizable entourage and typically required a lot of hand-holding, time-consuming briefings, and resource-intensive security measures. Other than duties associated with the CODELS, which were viewed about as favorably as a migraine, officers were left alone to do their jobs.

Even if your organization's crisis doesn't involve a war zone, you still have frontline employees. Your "troops" are those employees who have to face the public and deal with your customers as if nothing out of the ordinary was happening internally. These employees are the ones you need to protect the most from the turbulence associated with an organizational crisis. Give them the information, the resources, and the shelter from the internal power struggles that they need to convince your customers that your organization is just as capable as ever to provide them with the service they expect. Give them the authority and the protection to continue to carry on your organization's core business.

Protecting your frontline employees is related to a couple of other crisis management strategies:

- Employees who are protected from internal strife can more effectively **focus attention and action outward instead of inward.**

- Protecting your employees on the ground allows you to **redirect and refocus resources** in a way that is transparent to your customers, who expect service as usual.

CRISIS MANAGEMENT STRATEGY 8: CREATE LOYALTY BY INSPIRING IT AND TRUST BY EARNING IT

I saved this strategy until the end, because it doesn't truly fit here. For starters, this final strategy isn't really an independent line item. Rather, it is the culmination and the aggregate effect of using the first seven strategies described in this chapter. Managers who faithfully demonstrate the first seven strategies will, by definition, inspire loyalty and earn trust.

Moreover, inspiring loyalty and earning trust is not a concept unique to the clandestine world. In any industry, loyalty is created when employees see that senior management continues to work for the cause, rather than pulling the ripcord on the golden parachute at the first hint of crisis. Trust is earned when employees observe management communicating honestly and following through consistently.

Although these concepts are not unique to the clandestine world, I think that the CIA's response to 9/11 epitomizes both the application of the strategies and the resulting benefits.

I've already described the organizational turmoil within the CIA after the terrorist attacks, as well as the personal sacrifices and the long hours undertaken by officers. It truly made a difference that the grueling pace, the difficult working conditions, and the health and safety issues were borne equally by the most junior and the most senior members of the agency. I may have picked up a nasty intestinal parasite during my war zone travels (true, alas), but even in the throes of the worst abdominal cramps I knew full well that I had it easy compared to George Tenet's public grillings before Congress. The—ahem—unpleasantness did *not* sink to the bottom at the CIA.

Furthermore, the organizational trust that was built extended far beyond the clandestine service. The CIA *needed* to be a trusted organization post-9/11, since it was calling for unprecedented favors and support from nations all over the globe. Individual officers on the ground also relied on a trustworthy reputation when they made commitments to tribal leaders and warlords in Afghanistan for support, information, and protection. The atmosphere of loyalty and trust trickled outside the walls of the CIA, and influenced individual transactions, conversations, and commitments. In chapter 5, I described trust as a currency that can be saved and spent. The surplus of trust built up by the CIA during its response to 9/11 turned out to be just as valuable as the free-flowing cash.

Following the first seven crisis management strategies listed here can similarly build up a trust reserve to be doled out as necessary to get through difficult periods. The CIA—an organization that *truly* knows the meaning of crisis—is a testament to this fact.

Part Three

EXTERNAL APPLICATIONS

CHAPTER SEVEN

Making a Sale the CIA Way

Persuading a target to conduct espionage is much like making a sale. Some targets are uncomplicated buyers. They're the easy ones, of course. Their motivations are clear, they know what they want, and it doesn't take much persuading to get them to sign on the dotted line. A case officer's lucky day is when a volunteer with bona fide access to sensitive data comes marching right into the U.S. embassy, stating that he has important information to provide to the U.S. government. The case officer gets credit for "recruiting" a spy who volunteers, even if the officer did nothing but take notes.

A step up in difficulty are the potential spies who can best be described as coy. Ultimately, they're pretty sure that they're going to make a deal, but they want a little convincing—a little wining and dining. As a CIA officer gets closer and closer to a final recruitment pitch, the officer's cover intentionally starts to slip. Bit by bit, the questions become more direct and the meetings more discreet, until finally the officer and the spy just seem to fall into a clandestine relationship.

Some of the toughest potential recruits are those who seem to willfully refuse to acknowledge what is happening during the final acts of the recruitment cycle. These targets are the ones who might have already disclosed sensitive information, but they don't want to think of themselves as a "spy." It's one thing for people who fall into this category to hand over classified data now and then, but it is a far greater hurdle to persuade them to consciously commit espionage. They don't mind leaking information, but they don't want to think of themselves as traitors.

For this last category in particular, by the time a CIA officer makes a recruitment pitch, the officer's claim to be anything *but* a CIA officer is typically a very thin veneer. The officer has for some time been asking for detailed, sensitive information, making obvious efforts to keep meetings secret and avoiding communications via telephone or e-mail. Anyone paying attention would at least suspect that they were being wooed by an intelligence officer. In spite of this, stubborn targets tend to ignore the obvious, and they don't respond to subtle test pitches. These types of recruits wait until the officer has no choice but to make a blunt, explicit recruitment pitch. Of course, the more blunt the pitch ("I want you to steal secret information from your government in order to provide it to the U.S. government"), the easier it is to refuse. It takes a talented officer to maneuver an obdurate potential spy into accepting a daunting, direct proposal. An overly aggressive pitch will scare off the target, while a more subtle approach can drag on endlessly with no deal in sight.

Crafting the right approach depends entirely on the individual, the circumstances, and the chemistry between the officer and the target.

Sound familiar? It should. It's akin to any high-stakes sale—just with a twist of danger and a side of extra anxiety.

COLD PITCHES VERSUS DEVELOPMENTALS

CIA officers base most of their recruitments on the creation of a well-developed relationship. It takes time to establish the trust necessary to persuade someone to become a spy; potential recruits need to be thoroughly convinced that their handling officer will watch out for their safety and will honor commitments. The ideal recruitment pitch comes after months—or even years—of relationship building.

Sometimes, however, reality gets in the way of the process. In some circumstances a proper developmental effort just isn't possible. Your typical North Korean nuclear official, for example, doesn't get out much. He's not likely to spend his time vacationing in Mallorca or attending conferences in Los Angeles. Obviously, it's hard to develop a relationship with a person you can't even arrange to meet. In this type of situation, a CIA officer may resort to a "cold pitch." Cold pitches are less than ideal; they require a case officer to make a blunt appeal to the target with no opportunity to develop trust or rapport. They usually involve large sums of money, in the hope that a target will be sufficiently motivated by a generous financial offer. Not surprising, most cold pitches are declined. Would *you* agree to put your life at risk simply because a stranger approached you out of the blue and offered you a bundle of cash? Furthermore, an unsuccessful cold pitch can have consequences far worse than a simple refusal. If sufficiently offended or frightened by the pitch, a declining target may even report the CIA officer to local authorities. This can result in anything from diplomatic censure, to arrest, to being "PNGed" (a term referring to the act of expelling an officer from a foreign country and declaring him or her persona non grata, meaning that the officer can never reenter the country).

Like it or not, the corporate world also has to rely on cold pitches sometimes—for example, for consumer decisions that are made spontaneously, with little to no research or thought process. Or in the case of potential clients who are difficult to access or contact, a cold pitch may be the one and only opportunity to make a sale. A telephone interview for a coveted new job also requires a sort of cold pitch, since it is difficult to establish rapport during a brief phone call.

When possible, the developmental route is always the best—and not only because of the opportunity that it affords to develop trust and rapport. Just as important, developmental "time on target" is the only way to properly assess your target's vulnerabilities in order to help you craft the ultimate pitch with the greatest chance of success.

Depending on your industry and your product, you may be able to establish a unique one-on-one relationship with a potential customer. In other business situations, for example when products are sold through third-party vendors, developmental opportunities may be limited to the creation of a trusted brand image. No matter how little time you have, *some* development is always better than a cold pitch. The next section reveals techniques used by CIA officers to maximize developmental opportunities.

INCREASING THE ODDS

Because reality sometimes dictates that a sales pitch needs to be delivered before you have had the chance to thoroughly establish a trusting relationship, CIA officers use a number of techniques to maximize the chances that a pitch will be accepted. After all, in the clandestine world, an unsuccessful pitch can mean more than just time and resources wasted. Some failed pitches become full-blown international incidents, with charges, sanctions, and a one-way, do-not-pass-go ticket home for the embarrassed case officer. The following section provides eight techniques used by CIA officers to increase the odds that their target will accept a pitch. Each of these techniques is equally applicable in the corporate world and can help business professionals avoid being "PNGed" from a potential customer site.

Technique #1: Be a Chameleon

Whether you are selling *yourself* as the "product" during an interview or trying to broker a major deal, you can benefit from a thorough assessment of your potential customer. Do your homework up front, of course, and try to learn as much as possible about your target before you ever meet face-to-face. The most important assessment work, however, needs to happen during your initial contact.

Use the elicitation and corroboration skills that you developed while reading chapter 2 to complete a quick and dirty assessment. First, identify common interests or background elements that can help establish an early rapport with your target. ("You went to the University of Washington? Me too!") A *genuine* personal connection is invaluable for reducing some of the pressure and formality of a business interaction.

Next, figure out what type of customer your target is and what his or her vulnerabilities might be. Is he the type that will respond to a backslapping, expensive-dinner-buying approach? Or is she the type who will respond negatively to this tactic, mentally adding the cost of the dinner to the company's sale invoice? It goes without saying, of course, that you'd better have a whole arsenal of approaches at your disposal, ready to deploy quickly once you get a sense of your target's personality and vulnerabilities. This assess-and-adapt technique isn't sleazy or underhanded; it is simply a means of determining whether or not there is enough compatibility to justify a second meeting. As I will explain in the next point, for CIA officers a second meeting alone is well worth the mental quickstepping required to establish an early and enduring rapport.

Technique #2: Get a Second Date

CIA officers know that a patient, methodical approach is usually the best way to achieve a valuable recruitment. Often, then, an officer's one and only goal during an initial approach is to get a second meeting with the target. Even if the officer fails to obtain a shred of reportable data, a second meeting on the books is considered a success.

Why such a humble goal? Because getting a difficult target to agree to a second meeting means that you have met several important objectives. You have established a reason for continued contact. You have established enough rapport that the target is willing to spend more time talking to you. You have established an opportunity to meet again in a more controlled environment in which you can more purposefully advance your agenda.

This means that if you happen to meet your dream client on the golf course, don't try to finalize a deal by the eighteenth hole. Instead, use the chance meeting to broker a second, *focused* meeting. If you meet your dream boss in an elevator, forget the conventional advice to blurt out a rushed and all-encompassing "elevator pitch"; instead, use the ride to persuade her to schedule a proper interview. A major deal is too much to consider during a brief elevator ride together; a second meeting is not. When your ultimate objective is a high-stakes, long-term business relationship, don't be afraid to take time with the development process. Ultimately, it is worth the effort invested.

Technique #3: Lose the Canned Pitch

Ah, the canned pitch—remedy to a thousand different ailments. Nervous about public speaking? Many of us try to counteract those nerves by rehearsing a presentation over and over *and over* again until we could give it in our sleep. Been on the interview circuit long? Soon enough, the questions become predictable—and so do your answers. Pitched your product a thousand times already? You may find that not only have your words become robotic, but so have your jokes, gestures, and verbal tics. Delivering a difficult message to a difficult audience? Extensive practice can blunt some of the emotional cost to the speaker, but also some of the emotional appeal to the audience.

The canned pitch is a crutch that can do more harm than good. For starters, it is often painfully obvious. People who shift from casual conversation to an overly rehearsed soliloquy tend to give away the transition with a number of behavioral clues: they stand or sit up a little straighter, their language becomes either more formal or more unnaturally animated, they sometimes insert verbal artifices such as rhetorical questions ("have you ever wondered why . . ."), and the tone and pitch of their voice tends to change slightly. None of these things are bad per se, but all too often sincerity takes a backseat when your rehearsed pitch is given verbatim at the expense of responsiveness to your audience.

Worse yet, a canned pitch tends to put speakers on autopilot. Speakers in autopilot mode have a bad habit of ignoring audience cues that could prompt them to go in a different direction, or of not listening carefully to questions. A memorized interview response to an anticipated question can lead the speaker to miss the subtleties and nuances of the specific question. Do yourself a favor and ditch the canned speech in favor of knowing your product inside and out and giving yourself the ability to speak extemporaneously.

Technique #4: Maintain Input *and* Output

My first recruitment as a CIA officer was nerve-racking. I had gone through the recruitment cycle dozens of times in training, but this was the real deal. I was asking someone to quite literally put his life in danger in order to provide me with sensitive information. I was painfully aware that should he accept my offer, every piece of data that he collected for me, and every time he met with me, was at great personal risk to him. It's a lot to ask of someone, and I was nervous.

In an effort to calm my nerves I prepared an elaborate and flowery recruitment speech. I wanted him to know that I took his safety very seriously. I wanted to convey to him just how important his role would be and just how positive the impact of his cooperation could be. I wanted to address his concerns up front; I wanted to convince, reassure, and express gratitude all at once. I silently rehearsed this pitch continually during the long flight to our meeting destination.

Less than a minute into my little speech, my target glanced at his watch. A few seconds later he fidgeted. Then he glanced out the window. Then fidgeted some more.

The fact was, he didn't need the speech. He had long since divined where we were going with our relationship. He knew what I was asking, and he had already made up his mind to say yes. My flowery speech was unnecessary, and quite clearly annoying to him. I cut it short, cut to the chase, and we were toasting our new arrangement minutes later.

Would he have turned down my pitch if I had continued to

blather along as I originally planned? Probably not, but I'm still glad that I managed to gauge his reaction before I rambled any longer.

Too often people choose either input *or* output. They're either listening *or* they're talking. But if you are trying to make a sale, you need to maintain constant vigilance, even midspeech. The best speakers and the best salespeople can detect the moment when they begin to lose their audience. Watch for the signs as part of your ongoing assessment, and correct course instantly.

This does not mean that you need to obsequiously play up to your listener or kowtow meekly to your audience. In fact, depending on your strategy, you may be very well served by eliciting anger, skepticism, or some other seemingly negative reaction. The key is to know how you want your audience to react, and then to manipulate accordingly.

Technique #5: Analyze Your Own Weaknesses

Not even the best actors are infinitely versatile when it comes to playing a role. You can be as observant, responsive, and flexible as humanly possible, but there are always going to be situations in which you are, by nature of your appearance, your personality, or any other immutable characteristic, at a disadvantage. Perhaps you made a lousy first impression that your audience is not willing to forgive. Perhaps you remind the person who is interviewing you of her ex-husband. Perhaps you just can't manage to achieve personal rapport with your client, no matter how hard you try.

In the clandestine world, much thought is given to pairing the right officer with the right target. In most cases, the more similarities, the better. Matching language, ethnicity, gender, and professional background provides an automatic platform for the creation of a relationship. This is not, of course, always realistic, or even necessarily desirable. In fact, the overwhelming majority of targets

I worked against in my career were significantly older men with whom I shared neither religious nor ethnic background. And yet I made it work. I was able to work successfully with people from vastly different sociopolitical backgrounds with little to no difficulty largely because I acknowledged and took into account the targets' biases and probable reactions to a much younger, Caucasian, Western female.

On the other hand, there were also target populations that I was fairly certain I would never be effective against. My background, personality, appearance, and language capabilities were simply not target compatible. I therefore opted not to even pursue certain target sets because I knew that the odds were stacked against me before I even made initial contact.

I am definitely *not* advocating that readers pursue only opportunities that are a cultural/religious/ethnic/gender/favorite sports team match. Far from it, since I believe that some of the most advantageous business relationships exist between vastly dissimilar partners. I am, however, advocating that you know in advance how your audience is likely to respond to you, and that you have a plan for negating biases that are likely to work against you.

The key to self-awareness in this regard is to know how people tend to perceive you, for better or for worse. Think back to the times when you rubbed people the wrong way. Are there any commonalities? Do certain types of people tend to find you too brash, too arrogant, too passive, too quiet . . . too *anything*? Are there any similarities between circumstances in which you have felt misjudged? Are there any situations in which you tend to freeze up, get defensive, overcompensate for nerves, or otherwise react poorly?

If you lack self-awareness, you can do all the homework in the world to research your targets' backgrounds and vulnerabilities and still fail.

One of the best ways to gain awareness of how you come across to others is to conduct your own play-by-play analysis. When possible, have someone video record you during your sales pitch, presentation, or interview. If necessary, role-play the event if a live recording is not an option. Put the recording away for a few days without watching. After some time has passed, review your performance as critically as possible. While watching your video, try to understand which elements of your performance could be judged negatively. Don't just pick apart the technicalities; also try to understand how other people might respond to you on an emotional or interpersonal level. Are you likable? Professional? Interesting? Charismatic? Articulate? Authoritative? Or are you domineering, rambling, overly casual, or perhaps just visibly nervous? Do you mumble? Do you make eye contact? Do you frown? Dissect your performance down to the micro-expression.

If you can bear it, it also helps to have your most brutally honest acquaintance critique your video performance. Invite the worst—you need to know it. The whole purpose is to understand what tendencies, habits, and personality characteristics you need to compensate for with particular audiences. Understanding your worst helps you perform your best.

Technique #6: Sense Weakness in Others

CIA officers try to assess and learn targets' vulnerabilities as quickly as possible, in order to exploit them as systematically as possible. Here are just a few of the vulnerabilities I have taken advantage of in targets: a love of booze but a home in a dry nation; hatred of the regime in power; a strong desire to move to the United States; a polka-dot fetish (you'd better believe that I stocked up on clothing in that hideous print as soon as I learned this); the need for someone to listen to his political poetry; money; ego; money; ego . . . Let me repeat that a few more times: money; ego; money; ego . . . ego; ego; ego. Sense a trend?

It isn't terribly complicated. People like money—no big revelation there. People also like to be liked, they like to be heard, and they like to feel important. Generally speaking, focusing your development on these vulnerabilities is likely to at least get you moving in the right direction.

Business development, though, is not all about getting the customers to like their sales rep. It helps, but it is usually just one of many other factors. You can read all the books you want on how to get people to like you, but if your product isn't priced competitively or doesn't meet quality standards, you won't make many sales for all the charm in the world.

In the corporate world, then, detecting vulnerabilities is twofold. You need to identify both the business *and* the personal vulnerabilities of each of your targets. If you're lucky, the two will overlap. Usually you won't have such good fortune. You may in fact find yourself trapped between the personal and the corporate—woe to the sales rep with a client who is authorized to purchase only the cheapest of services, but whose personal weakness involves the costliest wining and dining.

Detecting business vulnerabilities is mostly about casting a wide net. You need to identify as many sources of information as possible in order to help you figure out how to direct your developmental efforts as early as possible. Background research goes without saying; the rest will depend on your industry. Various sources of information about your targets include former employees (or even current ones, for that matter), suppliers, resellers, online product reviews, and competition. Know what's going wrong with your target's business and be prepared to address this vulnerability. Be careful, though—it's hard to boost someone's ego if you are too busy pointing out his company's flaws!

Assessing vulnerabilities, whether business or personal, is simply one part research to one part intuitive assessment. Be prepared to act on whatever weaknesses you uncover—even if it means wearing an ugly polka-dot shirt to every meeting.

Technique #7: Regularly Rerecruit

A bit of a tongue twister, this one. It happens all the time—a CIA officer conducts a careful and thorough development of a target, pops the question, and gets a positive response. But then the newly minted spy goes home and starts to reflect on what he just agreed to do. He thinks of questions that he should have asked, but the case officer has instructed him not to call on an unsecure phone line. He wants to do some research, but he knows better than to use his home computer to search espionage-related topics on the Internet. He tells his wife, who begins to cry and accuses him of jeopardizing his family. He starts to have doubts—very serious doubts. Depending on just how cold his feet get, he may or may not even show up to the next meeting with his case officer.

Because of this phenomenon, which basically boils down to a highly emotional version of buyer's remorse, CIA officers are taught to always use the next meeting after the recruitment to "rerecruit." Valuable time is spent answering lingering questions, quelling fears, and erasing doubts.

The rerecruitment is repeated at regular intervals, and following any extraordinary events. A change in case officers, a close call while crossing the border, suspicious questions from a nosy colleague . . . all of these events merit time spent rerecruiting.

In the corporate world, rerecruiting need not be so emotionally laden. Instead, the rerecruitment process should consist of a regular examination of the business relationship and the reestablishment of interpersonal rapport. Don't take your clients or customers for granted, and don't wait until they threaten to move to your competitor before you rerecruit. Rerecruitment should be a regular, ongoing habit, even *within* your organization. We've all had bosses who seemed to sour on us over time or peers who grew distant; this can be fixed by regular efforts to rerecruit even co-workers.

Technique #8: Don't Negotiate

I originally considered writing an entire chapter on the clandestine approach to negotiations, but it quickly became apparent that it would be a very short one. You see, CIA officers don't negotiate. Or at least they avoid formal negotiations like the plague.

CIA officers tend to watch their American diplomatic counterparts, with whom they work closely, with bemused puzzlement. Quite unlike the clandestine world, the diplomatic world is full of complex protocols, formalities, resolutions, lengthy titles, and painfully regimented negotiations. Diplomats pride themselves on their debating skills and their knowledge of the United Nations' rules of procedure; they thrive in tightly controlled environments.

A clandestine service officer, on the other hand, starts to get antsy at the first sign of formality. When it comes to venues for important meetings, case officers prefer bars to boardrooms, and a restaurant table to a negotiating table. You'll never, ever get a case officer into a courtroom.

CIA officers do "negotiate" in the sense that they engage in discussions intended to produce agreements. But the clandestine version of negotiations looks quite unlike anything you will see in either the diplomatic or the corporate worlds. Here's a rundown of negotiation strategies, such as they exist, clandestine style:

▶ **Minimize the number of participants.** CIA officers prefer as few people to be involved in a decision as possible. More people mean more leaks, more risks, more biases, more arguments, more time, more possible naysayers, and more minds to change.

▶ **Aim high.** Why bother negotiating with an entire team when you can go straight to the top? Clandestine officers generally go directly to the committing official of any organization. Fortunately, CIA credentials give enough clout to permit officers to get on the calendars of even very busy, very prominent leaders.

▶ **Identify the decision maker.** The committing official is not always the decision maker. Make it your business to learn whether the top official in the organization with whom you are negotiating has a confidant or adviser. Whether because of lack of expertise, lack of confidence, lack of time, or lack of interest, senior leaders sometimes turn decisions over to a trusted subordinate. The person who actually makes the decision is the one you want to persuade.

▶ **Meet on neutral ground.** Agreeing to meet at your negotiating opponent's office makes it too easy for them to bring in other participants, such as legal advisers or assistants. Establish control by choosing a venue that is more conducive to small meetings. In fact, use the idea of a meeting on a sailboat as your gold standard. Participation is limited, privacy is maximized, the surroundings are conducive to pleasure and relaxation, and you maintain total control over the timing. Even if you can't *literally* procure a sailboat for your meeting site (not many of us can), always make an effort to woo your negotiating opponent before getting down to business.

▶ **Make an offer that can't be refused.** If you have a deep understanding of your opponent's vulnerabilities, you have the ability to make an offer that can't be refused. This tactic may involve putting together an offer that is so attractive that demurral would be foolish. Or it may be a polite version of arm-twisting. (No, legal folks, I am not advocating blackmail here, just an explicit awareness of consequences that would be unacceptable to your opponent, such as losing your business to a chief competitor.) Avoid the back-and-forth antics and posturing associated with formal negotiations by beginning and ending with the only offer you plan to make.

▶ **Follow through.** Whether you have made promises or threats, follow through. You may be back at the negotiating table sooner than you think; a reputation for bluffing will not serve you well.

▶ **Keep it positive.** In spite of the previous bullets that advocate the use of vulnerabilities, CIA officers use carrots far more often than sticks. An eager, willing partner is always preferable to a begrudging, reluctant one. Establish mutual benefits and shared gains whenever possible; the most productive negotiations always hinge on positive benefits rather than negative consequences.

Are you getting the sense that CIA "negotiations" sound quite unlike business negotiations? If so, you're right. You'd be amazed at the number of very important international matters that have been resolved over a cordial meal and a bottle of wine. As is the case in most clandestine affairs, clandestine negotiations are based on reputation, rapport, and strategic exploitation of vulnerabilities.

TRADECRAFT IN THE REAL WORLD

If you are reading this chapter and muttering to yourself that the book is emphasizing interpersonal matters over product or service differentiation, you are correct. CIA officers don't sell products. We don't claim to be better, faster, or more reliable than our competitors. We don't do product demonstrations or launch parties. We have impractical notions of finance, and we freely disregard laws that get in our way.

Clandestine service officers focus more on the sale than the product because the CIA obtains its product—secret information—*from* its targets. This circular business model simply would not hold up in the private sector.

If you take the information for what it's worth, though, you'll see the merits of this otherwise unorthodox approach to sales. The clandestine approach doesn't emphasize the product. It emphasizes interpersonal relationships, background information, vulnerabilities, reputations, and rapport. CIA officers go after unbelievably difficult targets, and using little more than an alias, some background research, a lot of chutzpah, a dose of charm, and ton of idealism, they manage to persuade people to do incredibly risky things.

CHAPTER EIGHT

Controlling Your Sources:
Supply-Chain Management Clandestine Style

In August 2009, Interpol conducted a massive raid on a cocoa plantation in Côte d'Ivoire, resulting in the rescue of fifty-four children who had been purchased for use as slave laborers. The children, who were as young as eleven years old and had been taken from seven different countries, had been forced to live and work in brutal conditions; they received no salary or education.

Ivorian cocoa is used by most of the world's major chocolate companies.

Because of a history of exploitation in the cocoa industry, a well-publicized labor rights initiative called the Cocoa Campaign has stepped up the pressure on candy companies to do more to prevent similar abuses. They have a compelling cause: the image of children enslaved for the purpose of cheaper cocoa is horrifying; the children's plight seems to come straight from the darkest of Grimm's fairy tales.

Clearly, this is the type of nightmare scenario that no company wants to be a part of.

Unfortunately, the children's horrendous experience is not uncommon; UN statistics put the number of child laborers at more than 200 million worldwide. Don't be lulled into believing that this is only a third world problem either; certain industries in the United States, including the dangerous meatpacking business, are regularly cited for underage employees. Other human rights and safety violations in the name of commerce show up disturbingly often in the news headlines. Scores of major Western companies in a wide variety of industries have been publicly lambasted for their suppliers' practices: Nike, Reebok, Gap, Starbucks, Firestone, Coca-Cola, Mattel, and Monsanto are just a few.

It's midnight—do you know what your suppliers are doing?

Unless you are an Amish furniture craftsman, your business likely relies on numerous suppliers and third-party service providers. Those sources have their own supply chains, and the subsources have their own suppliers . . . and so on. Within this extended supply chain, every degree of separation means a loss of control and oversight. With a loss of control and oversight, of course, comes all sorts of problems that you never in a million years thought you would have to deal with.

Supplier problems are not limited to child labor, nor are they exclusive to factories outside of North America. The U.S. Consumer Product Safety Commission directs dozens of nationwide product recalls every month, for reasons ranging from lead paint in children's toys to toxic ingredients in dog food to car engines that spontaneously burst into flames. There are an infinite number of ways that supplier problems can negatively impact your business.

And guess what? Customers don't give a damn that the issue was caused by your supplier's supplier's supplier. If *your* brand name is emblazoned on the finished product, then the problem is all yours.

THE . . . SOLUTION?

When I decided to leave my job as an investigator for the National Labor Relations Board, I interviewed for a position in a well-known consumer goods company that had been the target of copious negative publicity stemming from the labor practices of several of the company's overseas suppliers. Part of the job was oversight of the company's newly implemented supplier compliance program.

The job sounded interesting, and I eagerly asked questions about the compliance inspection program. I had my own ideas about how the labor practices of far-flung suppliers could be scrutinized, and I was curious about what steps the company had already taken.

I was stunned to learn that the inspection process relied heavily on the suppliers' local management. To begin the process, the corporate manager would contact the supplier's manager to initiate a "short notice" inspection. The company defined short notice as two weeks. As part of the inspection, the supplier was required to make employee representatives available for "confidential" interviews.

- **Problem #1:** Just imagine how much whitewashing can be done in two weeks.
- **Problem #2:** The supplier selected which employees would be interviewed.
- **Problem #3:** Interviews took place at the supplier's facilities.
- **Problem #4:** The supplier was responsible for providing the interpreter for the interviews.

Clearly, there wasn't much confidentiality involved. A handpicked employee representative being questioned on company property in the presence of an interpreter who is also in the employ of the supplier is not, of course, going to provide derogatory information about your supplier's practices. Not surprising, then, the company's first "inspections" had resulted in glowing reviews of supplier labor practices. Also not surprising, more than a decade later this company continues to struggle publicly with supplier problems.

I wish that I could say that this company's efforts were uniquely ineffective. Unfortunately, that is not the case.

CIA officers are proficient at identifying factors that impede their ability to obtain controversial data. All case officers know that, at a minimum, sources need to feel *safe* disclosing information, and *motivated* to tell the truth. The business world needs accurate, reliable information just as much as the clandestine world does. All the more reason, then, to borrow CIA techniques for getting the true story, even in difficult circumstances.

CORPORATE COMPLIANCE REALITY CHECKS

So, going back to the case of the Ivorian cocoa plantation, let's say that you are a candy maker with a good heart. You genuinely want to ensure that all of your raw ingredients come from suppliers who adhere to your corporate code of conduct. What's a kindhearted chocolate maker to do to ensure that nothing untoward is happening at the plantations that produce his cocoa? Well, most companies rely on the following techniques to ensure compliance:

- Require suppliers to sign an agreement promising compliance with your corporate code of conduct, which pledges adherence to legal standards and ethical principles.

- Reality check: Any employer willing to use child slave labor will not hesitate for a moment to sign your code of conduct, and then go right back to business as usual. The reality is that corporate codes of conduct are voluntary, and strict adherence is low. Sorry, folks— the bad guys think that your corporate code is a joke.

- Require suppliers to complete regular self-assessments and self-report any instances of noncompliance with corporate code of conduct.
    - See above reality check. I wouldn't even include this item, which I find ludicrous, except for the fact that it is actually used by a number of very large, successful corporations. Really, readers—let's not be naïve. Self-reporting is *not* an effective solution.

- Require suppliers to provide documentation for all employees to prove compliance with labor and employment laws.
    - Reality check: Documentation, particularly from foreign countries, can easily be falsified. In the case of the Ivorian cocoa factory, the children were obviously not "on the books"—they weren't even getting paid!

- Conduct routine inspections of supplier facilities during site visits.
    - Reality check: All evidence of wrongdoing will be gone long before you arrive for your quarterly site visit, and violations will resume within a matter of hours after your departure.

- Hire one of the external auditing firms that offer compliance inspection and certification services, including "surprise" inspections.
    - Reality check: Although some of these firms brag of consultants with law enforcement backgrounds, un-

scrupulous suppliers can easily evade most of their checks. Imagine the sight of a carload of American business consultants barreling down the dirt roads toward a remote African cocoa plantation. They don't exactly blend. You may pay a lot of money for their reports, but I promise you that they were spotted long before they could obtain evidence of wrongdoing. (By the way, that they likely made reservations at one of few nearby business-class hotels, hired local drivers, and hired local interpreters also means that their presence was announced long before they even arrived in country.) The Interpol raid on the Ivorian plantations was successful because it involved *eight* teams of *local* law enforcement officers who simultaneously raided the facilities in question; additional officers blocked the roads surrounding the plantations and searched cars for additional victims. Your expensive auditing firm is not likely to do this.

- Offer whistleblower awards for verifiable reports of noncompliance with corporate standards.
    - Reality check: Although well intentioned, this method can result in an avalanche of claims from disgruntled former employees, competitors, and outside rumormongers. There may very well be genuine reports mixed in there too, but the time and resources required to separate the false claims from the legitimate ones will be overwhelming.

You're getting the point. In many industries and in many parts of the world, conventional methods of monitoring supplier compliance are useless. So let's go back to our example of the kindhearted chocolate maker. If he truly wants to know whether something is amiss at his supplier's facilities, he has only one surefire way to find out: human intelligence.

Like the CIA, businesses can be well served by intelligence networks. Recruiting a single well-placed informer can provide far more information than a stack of monthly reports of questionable accuracy. The following section provides tips and techniques used by CIA officers to establish reliable intelligence networks than can be worth their weight in gold.

SOURCES WITHIN SOURCES: BUILDING YOURSELF A SUPPLIER INTELLIGENCE NETWORK

If your business relies heavily on suppliers or subcontractors, you have already relinquished control. After all, part of the reason companies choose to outsource is because they don't *want* responsibility for every detail and task. Because relinquishing control does not, however, always relinquish liability, it is imperative that you address problems quickly and directly. Whether you are trying to get to the bottom of chronic quality problems, head off costly delays, or ensure that your supplier is adhering to proper labor standards, you need real-time insight into your supply chain.

You *could* rely on self-reporting from your vendors. You *could* choose to conduct formal, scheduled inspections. You *could* chat with employees in break rooms and hope that the plant manager breathing over your shoulder won't discourage them from telling you the truth. You *could* rely on the monthly reports.

If, however, conventional means of monitoring your suppliers are failing you and you *really* want to understand the ground-truth realities at your supplier facilities, you need to create an intelligence network that extends throughout your supply chain.

For the purposes of this chapter, let's assume the most difficult scenario: multiple suppliers, each of whom uses a variety of subcontractors, located in remote areas of the world, and a workforce with whom you do not share a common language. It only gets easier from here! If your supplier happens to be located just down the street, then just take what you need from this section. The techniques work even if your "supplier" is simply a different department down the hall.

To start, an intelligence network needs—of course—spies. The ideal person to report on the realities of your supply chain is someone who:

1. Has access
2. Has motivation
3. Has the ability to communicate with you
4. Has proof

Not coincidentally, these are the same characteristics that CIA officers look for in potential spies.

I. Access. If you are trying to understand production control issues, it doesn't make sense for you to recruit a spy who works in the payroll department. If you are trying to confirm that your supplier isn't using child labor, it doesn't make sense to recruit the night watchman as a spy. The ideal source of information is a person who has access to the people, the records, and the plans that you need to know about. Depending on the complexity of your supply network, you may need multiple sources, each with unique access.

2. Motivation. Your sources will understand just as well as you do that if they produce enough derogatory information about your supplier, you are likely to terminate your business relationship and choose a new vendor. That, of course, would mean that your sources may very well be out of a job if their employer is forced to cut back in the face of your lost business. It is often in the best interest of employees, then, to toe the party line and report that nothing is amiss.

Because of this self-protection bias, you need a source who is motivated to provide you with the truth. Motivation may come in negative guise; your best source could be a disgruntled former employee with an ax to grind. Conversely, your best source may be a member of junior management who is willing to take the risk of becoming a whistleblower for a shot at a job within *your* company. It is important to be acutely aware of your sources' motivations, however, since their versions of "the truth" may be skewed by their reasons for cooperation.

3. Communication. If your source discovers information that you need to know on an immediate basis, will he or she be able to get you the data quickly and safely? CIA officers receive extensive training in clandestine communications, and they have access to all sorts of Hollywoodesque technology to help. Corporate spies don't usually require much in the way of bells and whistles, but you may need to go to some effort to enable your source to report back to you. This may involve managing language barriers, lack of Internet access, limited ability to make international phone calls, and time zone differences. Even face-to-face meetings may be impossible; if your supplier is located in a remote area, there may be no hotels nearby in which to hold a meeting. Your appearance at a source's home in an impoverished barrio would certainly draw attention, and your source may not have transportation to meet you out of the area.

Unfortunately, I don't have a one-size-fits-all communication plan to offer to you; no such plan exists. Every spy requires a unique and personalized communications strategy to get you the information when you need it. Work with your source to establish a context-specific communication plan that allows you to obtain critical information immediately.

4. Proof. You wouldn't terminate a contract over a rumor, so the members of your intelligence network need to be able to substantiate their reports. Unfortunately, your sources may need to go to considerable risk to back up their claims. When possible, you want your spies to clandestinely obtain photos, copies of lab reports, copies of personnel records, or any other incriminating data. If you are running the intelligence network, however, then *you* are responsible for giving your sources the technology and the training necessary to obtain proof in a way that does not jeopardize their safety or livelihood.

If this is all starting to sound a little too cloak-and-dagger to you, recall the above example of the enslaved child laborers discovered working at the Ivorian cocoa plantation. It is unlikely that the major candy companies had any inkling that one of many sources of raw ingredient was involved in such abusive practices. However, the fact that cocoa produced by slave labor made its way into the candy companies' products means they now share some of the responsibility to prevent such atrocities in the future. You'd better believe that it would have been in the candy companies' best interest, both from a moral and a publicity standpoint, to have known about the problem before they learned about it from an Interpol press release.

THE RISKS

I would be remiss if I didn't at least acknowledge the risks associated with using human intelligence collection techniques in international business. Although you may not break any laws by establishing sources to give you the inside scoop about supplier practices and problems, the application of clandestine methodology in the corporate world should always be done carefully, and with advice from legal counsel. But even if your activity is strictly legal, there are still risks:

▶ **Embarrassment.** Whoops, you just tried to recruit an internal source to report on your supplier, and it turns out that he's the plant manager's cousin. Not only does he turn down your "consultancy" offer, but he also reports your pitch to his cousin and the rest of the supplier management team. Needless to say, this is not going to have a favorable impact on your future business dealings.

- Avoid this by scrupulously researching all possible candidates and thoroughly evaluating their access, motivations, and relationships to key players. Never try to recruit a source without doing your homework! Also, try "soft pitching" first, when possible—this involves recruiting in baby steps. Give noncontroversial assignments first, then build up to the real tasks gradually, all the while assessing your source's willingness.

▶ **Risk to your source.** What happens if your source gets caught while trying to take photos of unsanitary conditions at your supplier's facilities? He loses his job, of course—at a minimum.

- Avoid this by anticipating risks, and give your sources adequate training and resources to avoid detection. See chapter 3 for more information about business counterintelligence techniques that can protect you and your sources.

▶ **Double agents.** Being a double agent is even more lucrative in the private sector than it is in the clandestine world. After all, if your newly recruited spy reports back to his employer, he may very well get a nice bonus for providing you with regular, falsely positive reports about your supplier's compliance practices.

- Avoid this by having multiple sources in different positions within your supply chain; this will allow you to corroborate reports.

▶ **The truth hurts.** Be prepared for the possibility that your new spy may report back on some truly egregious practices occurring at your longtime supplier's facility. After all, which is worse from both a moral and a legal standpoint: turning a blind eye to the *possibility* of misconduct, or doing business with someone you *know* to be involved in misconduct?

- Be ready and willing to act on reports of unacceptable supplier practices—whether that means terminating your business relationship or reporting your supplier to the authorities.

▶ **Jail.** I have advised readers repeatedly throughout this book always to obey the letter of the law. However, don't forget that some countries have blurred lines between state-run facilities and private enterprise. If this is the case, activities that may not violate business or trade laws may actually be considered espionage.

- Avoid this by *never* trying to build an intelligent network within any organization or entity with ties to the government. Espionage is something you never want to be charged with, no matter how skilled your legal team.

CREATING AN INTELLIGENCE NETWORK SAFELY AND LEGALLY

In the case of Ivorian cocoa plantations, I would advise cocoa end users to stop at nothing in the future to ensure that their suppliers are not engaged in abusive or unsafe practices. There are certain industries and certain parts of the world that have developed a reputation for repeatedly engaging in harmful practices. The garment industry, rug manufacturers, the diamond industry, and meatpacking companies, for example, have more than their fair share of labor problems. Other industries are chronically plagued with quality problems—as a parent, I am continually infuriated by the number of toys and baby products sourced from China that are determined to contain lead. When there is a history and a pattern of problems, not only should the buyer beware—the buyer should assume the worst until proven otherwise.

But what about the readers who aren't in one of the high-risk industries, and don't do business in parts of the world known to have problems? What if you just want to get an advance warning that your widget delivery is going to be delayed again? In truth, the creation of an intelligence network within your supply chain doesn't have to be a sneaky, risky affair. Particularly in the case of domestic suppliers, who are held to the same legal standards as you are, it doesn't really have to amount to much more than strategic networking, fueled by a healthy dose of skepticism. Running sources can be as simple as maintaining a positive relationship and regular contact with individuals who are willing and able to give you a heads-up when problems arise that may impact your business.

So for those of you who don't feel a need to issue clandestine communication plans or hold secret meetings with your sources, here are a few tips for being a more effective networker in order to be the first to know—spy lite, if you will:

1. Look for the people with dirty hands. I don't mean this in a derogatory sense. You want to know what's really happening in your supplier facilities? You need to have contacts outside of the executive offices. The people in the suits are not even necessarily aware of problems any sooner than you are. Know someone who actually *does* the work. Too often people obtain positions in management and never look back to the laboring ranks. That leads to an enormous blind spot—but one that is easily remedied.

When I went to Iraq in 2003 as part of the WMD search team, we still believed that there were weapons of mass destruction to be found. We interviewed senior scientists and politicians, all of whom denied the existence of a WMD program . . . and all of whom had been coached in propaganda. Because we could not rely on their rehearsed version of events, we started to look for sources who may not have been as well versed in the party line. We interviewed technicians, nurses, security guards, truck drivers, and people who just claimed to know someone who knew something. We interviewed exhaustively. Ultimately, it became clear that, lo and behold, there really was no secret WMD stockpile to be found. It wasn't until we had thoroughly explored all of the ranks, however, that we could be certain that we were hearing the truth and not just the cover story. The entire experience was enlightening for me in many regards; one of the lessons that I learned was just how differently people from different walks of life can interpret the same events and facts.

2. Learn a new language. It's amazing how much information is lost in translation—and I'm not just talking about foreign languages. If you're in marketing, you need to understand the engineers. If you're in HR, you need to understand production. Every industry and every career path has its own jargon; mastering the "language" used by the people who can provide you with critical information makes you much more approachable when the need arises. If you are unlikely to understand the explanation, then people don't want to bother bringing you into the loop.

This, of course, holds true for foreign languages as well. If your company outsources extensively to South America, *trust me*—you will benefit tremendously from learning Spanish. Being able to communicate directly, instead of through the prism of a translator, is always beneficial.

CIA officers who speak Arabic are a hot commodity. Arabic is a difficult language for Americans to master, and true fluency takes years to acquire. I don't speak Arabic, but I have had the opportunity on many occasions to use interpreters to communicate with Arabic speakers. I have also had the opportunity to witness Arabic-speaking colleagues in action. There is a world of difference between the two experiences. Working through an interpreter results in stilted conversation, and the tendency is for both sides to speak to the interpreter rather than to each other. Not even the best interpreters (and skill level varies widely) can fully convey subtleties such as underlying humor or threats; you will always be limited to literal translations that leave much unheard. I watched in awe as my Arabic-speaking colleagues not only managed to exchange information, but also to develop rapport and cultural understanding in a way that I never could by working through an interpreter.

By establishing yourself as someone who speaks their language— whether technical jargon or actual idiom—you let potential sources know that you have the capacity to hear and to understand.

3. Be generous with favors. The clandestine world is not altruistic. It is, however, generous. CIA officers in the field are often in a position to broker introductions, to help out with visa or passport problems, and to intervene in minor legal problems. They do so generously—not out of the kindness of their hearts, but because such small favors, which require little effort, often come back in spades.

By becoming someone who is generous with favors, you actually build yourself a powerful platform. It's human nature to dislike the feeling of debt or obligation, so the majority of people who receive a favor from you will be eager to repay the act whenever possible. Today's kind gesture just may turn into tomorrow's inside tip.

4. Establish your authority. CIA case officers are not known for their low self-esteem—they are not a timid lot. After all, if you're the type to stammer and sweat when an armed customs officer aggressively demands to know why you're carrying such a large amount of cash into the country, you won't last long in the industry. The ability to coolly, confidently defuse a stressful situation is a critical skill.

As I've mentioned, my very first assignment after completing my clandestine service training was to get on an airplane to Kabul. I found myself, still in my twenties, regularly meeting with roomfuls of armed Afghan men, most of whom hadn't seen a nonrelative female without the cover of a burqua in many years. Yet even though many of these men literally had not looked directly into an unrelated woman's eyes for decades, not a single one ever treated me with so much as an ounce of disrespect. Why? I'm fairly certain that it was because I walked confidently into every meeting, offered my hand for a firm handshake, never demurred, and always led the conversation. Oh yeah—and I also made it clear that I controlled the money. These men, who were totally unaccustomed to conducting business with women, had no choice but to shrug off whatever cultural discomfort they might have felt and sit down to get to work.

In the context of establishing a network within your supply chain, the same behaviors apply. Make yourself known as the one who is paying the bills, the one who can terminate the contract at any time, and the one who won't tolerate any deception. This doesn't have to be done aggressively or insultingly; rather, let it be known via your demeanor, your position, and your actions. Even if your act is nine-tenths bluff, establishing yourself as an alpha figure makes it much harder for people to lie to your face.

SUPPLY-CHAIN INTELLIGENCE

Are you surprised by how much I am emphasizing behavioral techniques above anything 007-ish? The reality of the clandestine world
is that undercover work is far more psychological than technologi-
cal. You don't need gadgets nearly as much as you need the ability
to manipulate perceptions.

When the circumstances call for an aggressive approach toward
addressing supply-chain problems, like in the case of the Ivorian
cocoa plantations, then clandestine techniques such as infiltration
and recruitment of internal spies may be justified. When, however,
such aggressive tactics are uncalled for, a somewhat more passive
approach may be perfectly effective. In that case, using the techniques adopted by CIA officers to establish themselves in positions
that entice, invite, and encourage full disclosure can go a long way
toward getting you the information you need from *all* of your
sources.

CHAPTER NINE

Spy Versus Spy: Dealing with Competition

During a clandestine meeting that had taken several months to arrange, one of my high-priority assets happened to mention that he was traveling to Paris the following week. "Oh?" I asked, instantly on alert. "For work or for pleasure?" This was an individual whose job did not allow him much opportunity to travel, so a trip to Paris was definitely unusual.

It turned out that the journey was a little of both. A mysterious French businessman had invited him on an all-expenses-paid trip for the ostensible purpose of a very brief business meeting. My asset wasn't entirely clear about the purpose of the meeting, nor did he really care; he had accepted the invitation solely because he had always wanted to visit the Louvre. The asset was an intelligent, educated man, but he was also stunningly naïve. I was not, however, quite so naïve, and a few more questions gave me all the information I needed. It was painfully clear to me that the French contact was an intelligence officer using an aggressive but well-known recruitment strategy. As I carefully picked apart all of my asset's conversations with the man, it also became clear that he had already revealed way too much.

I was concerned about my asset's safety, because even unwitting involvement with *any* intelligence officer added to the risk that his clandestine relationship with the CIA would be revealed. I was also furious on a more personal level. Someone had dared encroach on *my* turf! He was my asset, damn it, and everyone else had better just keep their grubby hands off. I instructed the spy to immediately cease all contact with his French suitor and to cancel his "business meeting." He sulked briefly, but agreed to do as I requested.

I sighed heavily after the meeting, thinking to myself, "Headquarters is *not* going to like this."

So you see—CIA officers have to deal with pesky competitors horning in on their business too. The clandestine world is a small community, and there are only so many high-priority targets to chase. In fact, it is not unheard of for top-tier targets to "shop around" in search of the best deal. Perhaps Mossad is offering more money. Or maybe MI6 is willing to consider offering expedited British citizenship. Can the CIA top their offers? As you can probably guess, this sort of bidding war can get very messy, and it is in everyone's best interest to sort things out quickly before the entrepreneurial target gets himself arrested, or worse. Rivalry and turf battles in the intelligence community, however, are a constant fact of life.

This is the chapter of the book where I have to tread most carefully. CIA officers are well versed in dealing with competition; after all, it is part of the clandestine service's mission to penetrate and sabotage other nations' intelligence functions. However, the vast majority of the techniques used by the CIA to deal with "the competition" are not at all conducive to the business world; in fact, they'd probably land you in jail fairly quickly. So I had to think long and hard about what a former CIA officer could offer you in the way of advice on this topic without crossing any legal or ethical lines. Ultimately, I decided that while I won't tell you how to clandestinely enter your competitor's facilities, sabotage a rival's new product release, or capture your foes' electronic communications, I *can* teach you the strategy and planning process used in the clandestine world to deal with competition.

IN-HOUSE COMPETITION

In an ideal work environment, you value your colleagues and respect your management. You may have developed friendships and camaraderie within your peer group, and you may seek guidance and mentorship from those co-workers with more seniority than you. If you enjoy such an idyllic work environment, or even if you just tolerate your mostly satisfactory job, it may not have occurred to you to create a dossier of sorts on your colleagues. Doing so may even feel mercenary and devious.

Get over it.

Your most talented, hardest-working, most gregarious, best-liked co-workers are your biggest threats.

That might sound a bit nasty, but the fact of the matter is, you are constantly being compared to your colleagues when it comes to decisions about promotions, bonuses, or career-enhancing opportunities. There's no need for you to do anything dastardly with the information you collect about your peers. Opportunities for advancement are finite, though, so it behooves all of us to identify and analyze our individual competition *within* our organizations. Use the following analytical framework to better understand where you fall in the organizational pecking order and how you can improve your chances for advancement:

I. Start at the top. To improve your professional trajectory, you need to understand your organization's leadership. The CIA has an entire analytical department dedicated exclusively to leadership analysis. Does this sound interesting? If so, the agency is hiring! The job description for leadership analysts is posted on the agency's public Web site. It states that leadership analysts

> produce assessments of foreign leaders and other key decision-makers in the political, economic, military, science and technology, social and cultural fields. These assessments are prepared at the request of senior U.S. policymakers in the executive and legislative branches to help them understand and deal with their foreign counterparts.

The assessments produced by the leadership analysts are used by policy makers to more effectively craft negotiating strategies, to understand vulnerabilities, and to predict behavior. You'd better believe that the president of the United States never goes into a meeting with a foreign leader without knowing what type of reception and response he is likely to receive. Even small personal details, such as knowing in advance about a foreign leader's dietary restrictions or rocky marital status, can help U.S. leaders avoid embarrassing errors of diplomacy.

Some of the leadership assessments compiled by the analysts are dry and dull—they can be based on anything from a detailed examination of decades of legislative decisions to minutiae gleaned from legal or financial records. Other assessments read like tabloid magazines—they can include tawdry details ranging from sexual proclivities to mental health assessments. The assumption behind the analysis is that foreign leaders' decisions and actions are influenced by their previous experiences, their personal vulnerabilities and foibles, and their psychological tendencies.

You may not have access to the same amount or type of data as the leadership analysts, but you'd be surprised at how easy it is to compile a meaningful assessment of the leaders of your own organization. After all, you interact with them, you read their internal communications, and you listen to their speeches. You see how they dress, what they drive, and what hours they keep. You see who they choose to fill positions of trust and responsibility, and you see who they hire and fire. It's as easy as watching and learning—all of the data that you need to complete your analysis can be collected in plain sight.

To truly understand your in-house competition, you need to be able to identify who your organization's leadership considers to be your competition. You may think that the guy in the cubicle to your left is the smartest, most diligent employee in the company (well, second to you, of course), but we all know that, unfortunately, intelligence and hard work don't necessarily have anything to do with professional success (long live the Peter Principle!).

To complete your leadership assessment, observe and analyze your organization's decision makers with the intention of answering the following questions:

- What are the characteristics of the people in the leader's inner circle?
- Who does the leader reward for successes?
- Who does the leader blame for failures?
- What are the differences between the people the leader has promoted from within and the people the leader has hired externally?

By studying your organization's senior leadership, as well as the leaders' prime influencers, you can assess what types of attributes and accomplishments tend to be rewarded. We all hope that our management will consider talent, intelligence, and dedication above all else, but the reality is often decidedly more complicated. Some senior executives demonstrate near-exclusive loyalty to former co-workers from previous organizations—they are the ones who bring entire staffs with them from their prior company. Others tend to surround themselves with people just like themselves (the so-called yes-men). Some value personal relationships over technical skills; others hire by "pedigree"—they insist that their subordinates come from prestigious universities and have previous experience working at prestigious firms.

Building a profile of your organization's leadership allows you to identify the characteristics of those who are fast-tracked into the positions that *you* want, and allows you to emulate the behaviors that may enhance your own career path—or at least to avoid the behaviors that are viewed unfavorably by your organization's leader-ship.

2. Study your rivals. At the risk of sounding a tad Sun-tzu here, a clear understanding of your rivals is critical to success. First you need to identify your competition, using the success criteria gleaned from your leadership assessment. After all, corporations are keenly aware of their competitors—shouldn't you be just as aware on an individual basis? Identifying your competition allows you to ad-dress the shortcomings that your organization's leadership sees in you in comparison to your rivals.

Identifying and analyzing your rivals does *not* mean that you should engage in overt competition. Far from it, in fact. Among your rival group will always be individuals who, by virtue of skill, luck, or personal connection, will ascend faster than you. These peers of today, then, may turn out to be your management of tomorrow. Rather than striking them as a hypercompetitive, back-stabbing shark, it behooves you to gain their respect while you are still operating as peers.

The CIA similarly seeks to identify individuals likely to be promoted quickly when it engages in what are called "seeding" operations. In a seeding operation, a clandestine relationship is developed with a person who may not be in a position of power or access *today,* but is deemed likely to rise into an important position in the future. Because it is often easiest to establish contact, and then ultimately to recruit individuals who are not yet ensconced in positions of power, CIA officers invest a great deal of time and resources into recruiting these future leaders in the hope that their predictions of future success will come true.

You can engage in your own seeding operation by working as hard to earn the trust and respect of your fast-tracking peers as you do with your management. Whether a person is invited onto the fast track because of skill, personal connections, or pedigree, establishing a relationship with a high-potential colleague while you are still peers gives you an added edge when your target gets promoted into a position in which he or she has the ability to reach back and bring you along for the ride.

3. Build an empire. I don't care if you work in the mailroom—everyone needs an empire of their own. By empire, I mean an entire system of individuals who are watching out for you. Too many competitive individuals look only skyward as they make their way up the organizational ladder; worse yet are those people who use the "kiss up, kick down" style of management that makes them hated by everyone whose shoulders they've ever trampled on.

Conversely, the best CIA officers as well as the most effective executives know that valuable information can come from highly unexpected sources. In fact, most intelligence services in the world maintain large networks of "support assets" whose value comes *not* from access to sensitive data but from their ability to do some of the behind-the-scenes work critical to a successful espionage mission. Support assets are the ones who maintain safe houses for clandestine meetings, purchase disposable cell phones for untraceable communications, or check secret message drop sites. A small subgroup of CIA support assets is used solely for the purpose of alerting a handling officer in the event that some kind of trigger occurs; this type of asset may be on the books, for example, to alert the CIA when a particular ship comes into port, or when a particular individual is seen engaging in suspicious behavior.

Support or alert assets are not usually prominent individuals; they are more likely to be sympathetic, low-profile, often low-ranking individuals whose value lies more in unobtrusive proximity to information than in inside access to secret data.

In the corporate world, having a network of access agents may mean that you get the computer upgrade first, that your messages are placed at the top of the in-box, that you are able to cut through bureaucracy more effectively than your colleagues, or that you get the office closest to (or farthest away from, depending on your preference) the boss. Having a network of alert assets means that you are discreetly notified *before* someone gets fired, that you know in advance about upcoming opportunities, or that you get a heads-up that today is *not* a good day to approach the boss with a request. These little favors and tips can be tremendously valuable, and can give you a strong competitive edge against your in-house competition.

So don't forget where you came from as you rise in the corporate ranks, and don't be reluctant to befriend the receptionists, valets, assistants, and janitors of the world. You never know what you might learn from your empire.

Anyone in the corporate world can emulate the CIA's strategy of

360-degree intelligence collection by studying their company's leadership, analyzing their peers, and building a network throughout their organization. This strategy sets you up for success and career ascension by helping you to become the go-to person when the organizational climate shifts, assisting you to establish a reputation as someone who always seems to be a step ahead, and giving you the ability to benefit from the successes and avoid the mistakes of those who came before you.

It goes without saying that none of this will make a difference (or at least it will make a much smaller difference) if you can't perform the basic functions of your job with a minimum level of competence. Assuming an acceptable level of expertise and effort, though, this method will allow you to work your way through the briar patch of your organization's culture in a way that mere technical proficiency does not.

EXTERNAL COMPETITION

So, how badly do you want to know what your competitor's next move will be? Given that this book is not a corporate espionage how-to manual, I am once again going to avoid all topics that could land either one of us in jail. The clandestine world's analytical models and strategies, though, apply just as well to the study of external competition as they do to internal competition.

1. Study the competition's MO. Although there are plenty of universal techniques and strategies in the clandestine world, every intelligence agency around the globe also has its own distinct modus operandi. There are the "gentleman spies" of the world who conduct mild, almost polite operations. There are also the thugs, who employ as much brute force as they do clandestine tradecraft. Certain countries have state-of-the-art technology; their advances in bio-metrics and crowd analysis make undercover officers and fugitives alike break out in a cold sweat. Other countries rely on cheap labor; they seem to have a surveillance officer posted at every street corner and in every hotel.

In order to operate safely, undercover CIA officers need to be familiar with the MO of the intelligence service in every country they visit. A case officer should always utilize good tradecraft, of course. In certain parts of the world, however, extra precautions are necessary in order to avoid detection. Based on a careful study of a country's intelligence practices, a case officer can make educated guesses about where surveillance units are likely to lurk, which ho-tel rooms are likely to be bugged, and which airports should be avoided at all costs. The information used to make these critical predictions comes from penetrations, analysis of past practices, and a thorough understanding of the current state of technology in use by the various intel services.

Private-sector organizations also have predictable patterns of be-havior. A company's MO might vary in the case of a drastic change in management, breakout technology, or an intentional reversal of strategy. Barring these rare events, however, it is possible for you to reasonably predict how the competition is likely to respond in a particular situation.

Identifying your competitor's MO requires a thorough under-standing of your rival company's history, a comprehensive leader-ship analysis, and awareness of important personnel changes. Generally speaking, you will find that the past predicts the future. Organizations are run by people, and people are complicated crea-tures. Because of this, human behavioral prediction models are im-precise at best. However, organizations are, by nature, resistant to change. This means that knowledge of your competition's history plus an awareness of potential triggers of change can help you predict your rival's next move . . . which should, of course, influence *your* next move.

2. Exploit your rivals' changes. CIA officers overseas put in a lot of overtime whenever there is a regime change in the country to which they are posted. Even if the new leadership is ostensibly friendly to U.S. interests, drastic changes in control are carefully scrutinized, and case officers scramble to collect intelligence on the new players in the game. This is because even when a new leader is a known entity, a change in power often results in dramatic organizational changes. New leaders are under pressure to be "different" and "better"; they are eager to put their mark on their position by making bold changes, whether or not such changes are necessary.

New leaders making drastic changes for change's sake can create weaknesses in an otherwise strong organization. Feathers get ruffled within the organization, while outside, customers get nervous, wondering whether they can expect uninterrupted service and quality. CIA officers *love* to exploit these cracks during regime shifts; it is far easier to recruit penetrations of a foreign government when people feel slighted or resentful of a headstrong new leader. Private organizations, similarly, have opportunities to pounce when the competition's leadership changes.

It's easy to think of organizations as faceless blobs, or as behemoth entities devoid of personality. And in truth, individual personnel changes rarely cause more than a ripple of difference, particularly in the long term. However, in the case of senior management changes in a competing company, be on high alert and ready to exploit organizational vulnerabilities that may appear as a result of an individual's actions.

3. Use denial and deception. The CIA uses denial and deception techniques to mislead rival intelligence services; the goal is to keep the other service spinning with false leads and incorrect information so that the *real* work can go on undetected. I don't encourage readers to do anything unethical or unsafe, *but* if you become aware of a competitor's efforts to commit corporate espionage against your company, you have a golden opportunity. Rather than immediately firing the mole, investigating the leak, changing your hacked e-mail account's passwords, or otherwise shutting off your rival's source within your company, consider using the source *against* your scheming competitor. When you control the information being leaked, you gain control over your rival's responses.

4. Build an alliance. Everyone knows that building relationships is a critical part of doing business, but most organizations view relationship building as a function belonging only to sales and marketing. Instead of using relationships only to drive sales, consider the possible intelligence value of strong relationships with suppliers, consultants, legal and financial representatives, and any other organization that your company regularly comes into contact with.

The Central Intelligence Agency relies heavily on alliances with foreign governments—even those whom we are actively spying against. In the case of a crisis, or even an isolated, mutually beneficial opportunity, our rival intelligence services temporarily share resources and information that are critical to success. It may be a self-serving gesture in many cases, but who cares? Similarly, the CIA follows a duty-to-warn doctrine that requires agency officials to notify foreign governments when credible information is received about an impending threat of attack; the agency abides by this doctrine even in the case of enemy nations.

Building business relationships that may have nothing to do with sales can be beneficial in highly unexpected ways. If nothing else, the creation of alliances with external organizations gives you additional sources of information that can impact your business. At a certain level within every industry, it becomes a very small world. Your vendor may have once worked with your rival's new CEO, or the head of the consulting firm that you use regularly may be considering hiring someone from your competitor. The type of information that can be passed through industry alliances, wittingly or unwittingly, can provide a genuine business advantage.

Operating in a Competitive World

I t's a competitive world out there, and it can be tempting to play dirty—particularly if "fair" seems to be a foreign concept to your rivals. Playing hardball, though, tends to result in *all* of the players getting battered. In the corporate world as in the clandestine, it simply isn't worth the hit to your reputation (or your legal defense fund), no matter how tempting it is to bend the rules to get to the top.

I mentioned earlier in the book that integrity is a valuable commodity. Rather than emphasizing the negative aspects of dealing with competition in the clandestine world, then, I'd prefer that readers walk away with the notion that a solid reputation for integrity is far more valuable than any kind of dirty trick that an ex-spook can teach you.

Don't get me wrong—I'm not playing Girl Scout here. I highly recommend strong defensive counterintelligence practices, pristine security procedures, and the use of good tradecraft to protect your organization's interests. But today's rival can be tomorrow's ally. Responding to competition intelligently, perceptively, even aggressively can hardly be faulted. Using dirty tricks to gain a small advantage, on the other hand, can—and often does—come back to haunt you.

CIA officers may not face the same legal, logistical, or financial constraints that business executives do. They do, however, have goals, objectives, and aspirations, just like their counterparts in the corporate world. As someone who has spent time in both the spy business and in more traditional business settings, I have come to realize that many of the unique skills taught to CIA officers to help them achieve their mission are equally applicable in the private sector.

I have endeavored throughout this book to make it clear that I am *not* advocating corporate espionage or any type of practice that could be considered legally or morally questionable. I *am*, however, offering readers the rare opportunity to learn from the successful practices used by hardworking and talented CIA officers every day.

Overall, if I had to sum up the most important business lesson from the clandestine world, it would be this: there is information for the taking that can change the entire playing field for you and your organization. Getting this information is a matter of asking the right people the right questions in the right way. This may require manipulation of individuals and exploitation of both organizational and personal vulnerabilities. However, by adhering to firm ethical parameters, it is possible to use clandestine techniques to get ahead in the corporate world while still maintaining your integrity.

Acknowledgments

It's difficult to write acknowledgments when I can't name so many of the people I'd like to thank. But I do want to express my gratitude for those CIA officers who have been my mentors, my friends, my travel companions, my war zone roommates, and my colleagues. Your job presents more challenges and asks more sacrifices than most; it was an honor to serve with you.

I also want to recognize the team at Portfolio / Penguin for its patience and hard work—this book was a work in process for much longer than any of us expected.

Finally, I'd like to thank my mother for tolerating my globetrotting and thrill-seeking ways from such a young age. It's only now that I'm a parent that I realize what I must have put you through. May my children never give me as many gray hairs as I'm sure I have given you!

Index